USING

linkedin®

Patrice-Anne Rutledge

800 East 96th Street, Indianapolis, Indiana 46240 USA

Using LinkedIn®

Copyright © 2010 by Pearson Education, Inc.

ISBN-13: 978-0-7897-4459-3
ISBN-10: 0-7897-4459-7

Library of Congress Cataloging-in-Publication Data:
Rutledge, Patrice-Anne.
  Using LinkedIn / Patrice-Anne Rutledge.
    p. cm.
  ISBN 978-0-7897-4459-3
  1. LinkedIn (Electronic resource) 2. Business networks—Computer network resources.
3. Business enterprises—Computer network resources. 4. Job hunting—Computer network resources. I. Title.
  HD69.S8R88 2010
  658.3'1102854678—dc22

2010023419

Printed in the United States of America
First Printing: June 2010

Trademarks

Warning and Disclaimer

Bulk Sales

Que Publishing offers excellent discounts on this book when ordered in quantity for bulk purchases or special sales. For more information, please contact

U.S. Corporate and Government Sales
1-800-382-3419
corpsales@pearsontechgroup.com

For sales outside of the U.S., please contact

International Sales
international@pearson.com

Associate Publisher
Greg Wiegand

Acquisitions Editor
Michelle Newcomb

Development Editor
The Wordsmithery, LLC

Managing Editor
Sandra Schroeder

Senior Project Editor
Tonya Simpson

Copy Editor
Water Crest Publishing

Senior Indexer
Cheryl Lenser

Proofreader
Williams Woods Publishing

Technical Editor
Vince Averello

Publishing Coordinator
Cindy Teeters

Book Designer
Anne Jones

Cover Designer
Anna Stingley

Compositor
Mark Shirar

Media Table of Contents

To register this product and gain access to the Free Web Edition and the audio and video files, go to quepublishing.com/using.

Contents at a Glance

Table of Contents

About the Author

Patrice-Anne Rutledge is a business technology author and consultant who specializes in teaching others to maximize the power of new technologies such as social media and online collaboration. Patrice is a long-time LinkedIn member and social networking advocate who uses LinkedIn to develop her business, find clients, recruit staff, and much more. Her other books from Pearson Education include *Sams Teach Yourself LinkedIn in 10 Minutes* and *The Truth About Profiting from Social Networking*. She can be reached through her website at www.patricerutledge.com

Dedication

To my family, with thanks for their ongoing support and encouragement.

Acknowledgments

Special thanks to Michelle Newcomb, Charlotte Kughen, Vince Averello, Sarah Kearns, and Tonya Simpson for their feedback, suggestions, and attention to detail.

We Want to Hear from You!

As the reader of this book, *you* are our most important critic and commentator. We value your opinion and want to know what we're doing right, what we could do better, what areas you'd like to see us publish in, and any other words of wisdom you're willing to pass our way.

As an associate publisher for Que Publishing, I welcome your comments. You can email or write me directly to let me know what you did or didn't like about this book—as well as what we can do to make our books better.

Please note that I cannot help you with technical problems related to the topic of this book. We do have a User Services group, however, where I will forward specific technical questions related to the book.

When you write, please be sure to include this book's title and author as well as your name, email address, and phone number. I will carefully review your comments and share them with the author and editors who worked on the book.

Email: feedback@quepublishing.com

Mail: Greg Wiegand
        Associate Publisher
        Que Publishing
        800 East 96th Street
        Indianapolis, IN 46240 USA

Reader Services

Visit our website and register this book at quepublishing.com/using for convenient access to any updates, downloads, or errata that might be available for this book.

Introduction

Although professionals have always acknowledged the value of networking, today's economic climate makes developing a solid network even more critical. LinkedIn, the leading social networking site for professionals, is the ideal tool for maximizing the potential of an online network. LinkedIn currently has more than 65 million members worldwide, including executives from all Fortune 500 firms and President Barack Obama, and is growing rapidly. A new member joins approximately every second.

It's clear that today's technology has forever changed the way people find a job, promote their businesses, foster strategic partnerships, and develop their professional networks. Social networking continues to generate media buzz and mainstream appeal. According to a March 2009 study by Nielsen Online, participating on social networking sites is now more popular than reading email. But technology is just the enabler. The fundamental concepts of professional networking remain the same both online and off. Building relationships through mutual connections and trust is the foundation of success on LinkedIn just as it is in the real world.

This book is for anyone who wants to tap into the power of LinkedIn for professional reasons. LinkedIn connects you with a network of professional colleagues and enables you to maintain an online presence, find a job, recruit employees, promote your business, find clients and partners, get answers to professional questions, perform market research, and much more. It's a viable business tool that opens up new ways to connect with others who can help you achieve your business goals.

Using LinkedIn is designed to get you up and running on LinkedIn as quickly as possible. This book focuses on standard LinkedIn functionality. LinkedIn rolls out beta functionality and new features on a regular basis, so the features available to you might vary at any given time. The companion website to this book will help keep you updated on what's new with LinkedIn. For now, turn to Chapter 1, "Introducing LinkedIn," to get started with this powerful networking tool.

Who Is This Book For?

This book is for you if...

- You want to become productive on LinkedIn as quickly as possible and are short on time.

- You want to generate better results from your LinkedIn profile.

- You want to find a job or promote your business online, taking advantage of all that social networking has to offer.

- You're a visual learner and want to *see* how to use LinkedIn in addition to reading about it.

Companion Website

This book has a companion website online at http://www.patricerutledge.com/using-linkedin.

Visit the site to access the following:

- Book updates

- News about LinkedIn enhancements and features

- Other books and courses that might be of interest to you

Conventions Used in This Book

More than just a book, *Using LinkedIn* is tightly integrated with online video tutorials, audio insights, and other web-based content, which is all designed to provide you with a media-rich, customized learning experience not available through any other book series today. *Using LinkedIn* is a thorough resource at your fingertips.

Important tasks are offset to draw attention to them.

LET ME TRY IT

Tasks are presented in a step-by-step sequence so you can easily follow along.

SHOW ME   Media—Watch complex tasks performed in video tutorials.

TELL ME MORE   Media—Listen to audio interviews and sidebars from the experts.

Media and Support

The Using series lives online at www.quepublishing.com/using. Visit this site to register your book, gain access to the media files, and complete your learning experience.

This chapter introduces you to the basics of LinkedIn and shows you how to develop a strategy for success with this popular social networking site.

1

Introducing LinkedIn

LinkedIn (www.linkedin.com) is the world's leading social networking site for professionals, with many millions of profiles of members around the world. LinkedIn is expanding rapidly: A new member joins approximately every second. The site is extremely active with recruiters from recruiting firms as well as from major companies such as Microsoft, eBay, US Cellular, Kaiser Permanente, and L'Oréal, which makes it a prime hunting ground for job seekers.

Everyone from top CEOs to President Barack Obama has a LinkedIn profile. If you want to network for business on just one social networking site, LinkedIn is the site to choose.

In this chapter, you learn how to choose the right LinkedIn account for your goals and find exactly what you want on LinkedIn's extensive site. You can also listen to advice on making the most of LinkedIn and watch videos that show you how to sign up for a LinkedIn account, explore the LinkedIn home page, and navigate LinkedIn.

Understanding the Power of LinkedIn

Creating a professional profile and developing a solid network of connections on LinkedIn can help you meet many goals. For example, participation on LinkedIn can enable you to do the following:

- Find a job or recruit quality job candidates
- Develop your business by connecting with clients and partners and promoting yourself as a service provider
- Brand yourself online with a professional presence that demonstrates your expertise

 TELL ME MORE　Media 1.1—The Power of LinkedIn
Access this audio recording through your registered Web edition at
my.safaribooksonline.com/9780789745095/media.

Understanding the Key to Success on LinkedIn

The key to success on LinkedIn is to establish clear goals and ensure that your actions on the site work to achieve these goals.

For example, if your goal is to find a job through LinkedIn, you want to create a strong profile with keywords that attract recruiters. You also want to develop a solid network of professional contacts in your industry—the type of people who might hire you or who might provide relevant job leads.

On the other hand, if your goal is to find business leads and develop your platform as an expert in your field, you could use a different approach. A strong profile and network are still important, but you might also want to participate in LinkedIn Answers and LinkedIn Groups to promote your expertise among LinkedIn's millions of members.

Before establishing your goals, however, you need to understand the unwritten rules of LinkedIn. LinkedIn's focus is on developing a mutually beneficial online business network. With LinkedIn, you can stay in touch with your existing contacts and connect with other professionals who share your goals and interests. LinkedIn is not the place to amass thousands of "followers," engage in heavy sales tactics, or send spam-like communications. Keeping these "rules" in mind will help you develop a LinkedIn strategy that generates positive results in your professional career.

Understanding LinkedIn Account Types

LinkedIn offers several account types, including a free Personal account, three types of premium accounts, and three types of Job Seeker accounts. See Chapter 9, "Searching for Jobs," for more information about Job Seeker accounts.

All accounts offer the ability to do the following:

- Create a professional profile
- Develop a network of connections
- Search for jobs and people
- Send unlimited messages to your connections
- Receive unlimited requests for introductions and InMail
- Participate in LinkedIn Groups
- Participate in LinkedIn Answers

See Chapter 6, "Communicating with Your LinkedIn Network," for more information about messages, InMail, and introductions.

InMail is a private message from a LinkedIn member who is not your connection and has paid for the privilege of contacting you.

With a free Personal account, you can do the following:

- Maintain a maximum of five pending introductions to other LinkedIn users at one time

- View 100 profile results per search

- Save a maximum of three searches and get weekly alerts on those searches

You can perform and save targeted searches for people, jobs, companies, and other LinkedIn content. See Chapter 7, "Searching for People on LinkedIn," for more information about LinkedIn's search capabilities.

LinkedIn's free account offers so many powerful features that it should suit the needs of most users. Unless you specifically need a premium feature, try out the free account first before making the decision to upgrade.

Exploring LinkedIn Premium Accounts

Premium accounts offer you the ability to contact more people who aren't connected to you and are ideally suited to recruiters or people using LinkedIn as a business development tool.

LinkedIn's premium accounts enable you to

- Perform unlimited one-click reference searches

- Receive an OpenLink Network membership and receive unlimited OpenLink messages

- Send unlimited OpenLink messages

- Receive LinkedIn customer service responses within one business day

> The OpenLink Network is a LinkedIn premium feature that enables network members to contact each other without incurring additional fees.

Your choice of the specific premium account that's right for you depends on your need for InMail, introductions, and searches.

The Business account costs US $24.95 per month. With this account, you can

- Send three InMails per month
- Save five searches and receive weekly alerts on each
- Maintain 15 pending introductions at one time
- Create five Profile Organizer folders
- View 300 profile results per search

> The LinkedIn Profile Organizer enables you to save and organize profiles of interesting LinkedIn members in folders. For example, these could be people you're interested in recruiting for a job or potential business contacts. See Chapter 7 for more information.

The Business Plus account is priced at US $49.95 per month. With this account, you can

- Send 10 InMails per month
- Save seven searches and receive weekly alerts on each
- Maintain 25 pending introductions at one time
- Create 25 Profile Organizer folders
- View 500 results per search

The Pro account, at $499.95 per month, might interest power users. Pro users can

- Send 50 InMails per month
- Save 10 searches and receive daily alerts on each
- Maintain 40 pending introductions at one time
- Create 25 Profile Organizer folders
- View 700 results per search

If you need a higher volume of InMails and introductions than the available premium accounts offer, consider signing up for LinkedIn Talent Advantage (http://talent.linkedin.com), a suite of power solutions for recruiters.

Signing Up for LinkedIn

Signing up for a LinkedIn account is a simple, straightforward task. Figure 1.1 shows the welcome screen that greets you the first time you visit LinkedIn (www.linkedin.com).

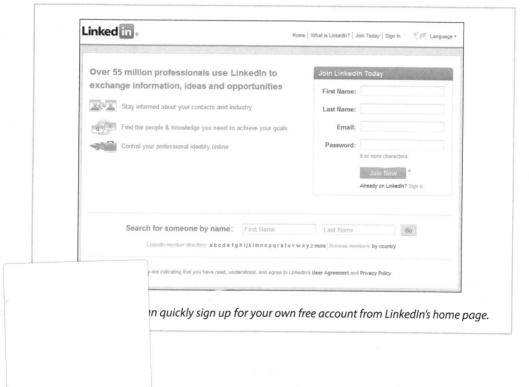

...n quickly sign up for your own free account from LinkedIn's home page.

Media 1.2—Signing Up for a LinkedIn Account
Access this video file through your registered Web edition at
my.safaribooksonline.com/9780789745095/media.

 **LET ME TRY IT**

Signing Up for a LinkedIn Account

To create your own LinkedIn account, follow these steps:

1. In the Join LinkedIn Today box, enter your first and last name, email address, and a password. Be sure to create a strong password. A password that contains a combination of uppercase and lowercase letters, numbers, and symbols provides the most protection.

> LinkedIn offers privacy controls to protect your business email address. Entering the email address that most of your business contacts use to communicate with you yields the best results when others try to connect with you by email on LinkedIn.

2. Click the Join Now button. The Let's Get Your Professional Profile Started page appears, shown in Figure 1.2.

Figure 1.2 *Enter your basic data to get started on LinkedIn.*

3. In the I Am Currently field, select your employment status from the options available. Options include the following:
   - Employed
   - A business owner
   - Looking for work
   - Working independently
   - A student

The selection you make in the I Am Currently field determines which of the following fields appear: Company, Job Title, Industry, Education, and Dates Attended. If one of these fields doesn't appear, it's because it isn't required for your job status.

4. Enter your company, if applicable. As you start typing, LinkedIn locates potential company matches from existing profiles. Choosing from an existing entry helps ensure that you and your colleagues are correctly linked by company.

5. Enter your current job title, if applicable.

6. If applicable, select the industry that best describes your professional expertise from a list of more than 100 options. These options range from popular professions (Accounting, Banking, Computer Software, Internet, Real Estate, and Marketing) to the more obscure (Dairy, Gambling & Casinos, Fishery, and Think Tanks).

7. If you're a student, select your school from the drop-down list or select Other in the list and enter your school name in the text box that appears. Also enter your dates attended to help you connect with current and former classmates.

8. Enter your country and ZIP code. Note that LinkedIn displays only your geographic region, such as San Francisco Bay Area, and not your actual ZIP code or city on your profile. If you live in a country outside the United States, the Postal Code field appears instead of ZIP Code.

9. Click the Continue button to open the Confirm Your Email Address page. On this page, LinkedIn prompts you to confirm your email address.

LinkedIn prompts you to search for your webmail contacts and invite them to connect. Doing so is optional at this stage. I recommend that you click the Skip This Step link for the remaining steps and complete this task after you've created your profile.

As a security measure, LinkedIn sends a confirmation message to the email address you entered when you signed up for an account. Click the link in this message to confirm. This ensures that the person who actually owns the email account signed up for LinkedIn and not someone else.

If you don't receive a confirmation message from LinkedIn, check your spam or junk mail folder. Alternatively, click the Request Another One link in the Confirm Your Email Address box on your LinkedIn home page to resend the confirmation.

Once you have a LinkedIn account, click the Sign In link whenever you visit the site to log on again with your primary email address and password. If you forget your password, click the Forgot Password? link on the Sign In to LinkedIn page to request a new one. If you always use the same computer to access LinkedIn, such as a home computer, you can remain logged in for up to 24 hours as a convenience.

When you first sign up for LinkedIn, you receive a personal account. To upgrade a personal account to a premium account, click the Upgrade Your Account link on the bottom navigation menu.

Finding Your Way Around LinkedIn

LinkedIn includes millions of pages of data, so knowing how to find your way around can help save you lots of time. Fortunately, once you understand the LinkedIn navigation structure and the best ways to use your home page (command central on LinkedIn), you should be able to quickly find what you're looking for.

Exploring the LinkedIn Home Page

Your home page appears when you log on to LinkedIn. Figure 1.3 shows a sample home page, which is the dashboard of your LinkedIn activity.

 SHOW ME   **Media 1.3—Exploring the LinkedIn Home Page**
Access this video file through your registered Web edition at
my.safaribooksonline.com/9780789745095/media.

The content on your home page is dynamic and is unique to your LinkedIn actions, network, and account settings. When you first create a LinkedIn account, the Build Your Network box on your home page encourages you to start connecting with your existing contacts. However, I recommend that you create your profile before completing this step. Why? Because when your contacts receive your connection request, you want them to view a complete profile, not an empty one.

See Chapter 2, "Creating Your LinkedIn Profile," for more information about creating your own profile. See Chapter 3, "Developing Your LinkedIn Network," for more information about building your LinkedIn network.

Figure 1.3   *Your home page is your main LinkedIn dashboard.*

After you create a profile and develop a network of more than 20 connections, however, LinkedIn enables you to close this box by clicking the Close (x) button that appears in the upper-right corner.

The left column of your home page includes only the Build Your Network box when you first sign up for LinkedIn. But after you create your profile and start developing your network, other items appear, such as the following content:

- **Inbox.** Displays a preview of your Inbox with links to the five most recent unread messages. If you don't have at least five unread messages, the preview displays the number of unread messages that are available. See Chapter 6 for more information about your Inbox.

- **Network Activity.** Displays the actions and activities of your connections on LinkedIn. These include updates, profile updates, new connections, and group updates, for example. You can also post your own updates in this section. See Chapter 5, "Maintaining Your LinkedIn Profile," for more information about updates.

Click the orange feed icon next to the Network Activity heading to open the LinkedIn RSS Feeds page where you can subscribe to your LinkedIn network updates and read them in a feed reader. See Chapter 4, "Customizing Your LinkedIn Experience," for more information about RSS and feeds.

- **Group Updates.** Displays recent group updates, including information about the groups your connections joined and comments and recommendations from fellow group members.

- **News.** Displays recent news articles about your company, competitors, and industry. You can also participate in discussions with your colleagues about news articles, recommend news to your colleagues, share news with your connections, or submit your own articles. The News section appears on your home page only if news is available for your current employer. If you're self-employed or work for a small company, this section might not appear on your home page.

- **Just Joined LinkedIn.** Displays links to new colleagues and classmates who have joined LinkedIn recently.

To customize the network updates that appear on your home page, click the Settings link in the top navigation menu and click the Network Updates link to open the Network Updates page.

The right column of your home page displays the following:

- A list of three people you might know based on your existing connections. You can click the Invite link to the right of their name to send an invitation to connect. If you haven't added any connections yet on LinkedIn, this option won't appear.

- An advertisement.

- The Who's Viewed My Profile? box. Click the See More link to learn more about the people who have viewed your profile. If you haven't created a profile yet or no one has viewed your profile, this option won't appear.

- Boxes for LinkedIn applications and features, such as Events, LinkedIn Answers, Jobs, and Amazon Reading List recommendations. LinkedIn uses the information from your profile to determine relevant content to display. For example, if you select Marketing as your industry, the content displayed should be useful to a marketing professional. See Chapter 12, "Enhancing Your Profile with LinkedIn Applications," to learn more about LinkedIn applications.

To remove a box that displays in this column, click the X button in the upper-right corner of the box. Some boxes include an Edit link that you can click to customize the data that appears. To add application boxes, click the Add an Application button at the bottom of the column to select from the available options.

Navigating LinkedIn

Navigating LinkedIn is a straightforward process once you understand its navigational structure. LinkedIn pages display two navigation tools: a global navigation bar at the top of the screen and a bottom menu of additional options.

 SHOW ME   Media 1.4—Navigating LinkedIn
Access this video file through your registered Web edition at
my.safaribooksonline.com/9780789745095/media.

The global navigation bar, shown in Figure 1.4, includes links to the most popular LinkedIn destinations, with drop-down menus offering additional options. Links on the top navigation menu include the following:

- **Home.** Return to the LinkedIn home page.

- **Profile.** Edit or view your profile and recommendations.

- **Contacts.** Manage, add, and import connections.

- **Groups.** View your groups, view a group directory, or create a group.

- **Jobs.** Perform an advanced job search or manage job postings.

- **Inbox.** View, send, and archive LinkedIn messages.

- **More.** Choose one of the following destinations from the drop-down menu: Companies, Answers, Learning Center, and Application Directory. This menu also includes links to your installed applications, such as Events or Amazon Reading List.

Figure 1.4   *LinkedIn's global navigation bar provides links to common tasks.*

A search box appears to the right of the global navigation bar. See Chapter 7, "Searching for People on LinkedIn," to learn more about LinkedIn search options.

Above the global navigation bar are several other links:

- **Add Connections.** Send invitations to potential LinkedIn connections.

- **Settings.** Customize the way you use LinkedIn.

- **Help.** Search LinkedIn online help.

- **Sign Out.** Log off LinkedIn.

The bottom of the LinkedIn screen links to additional menu options, including LinkedIn company information, the LinkedIn blog, language choices, LinkedIn tools, and premium features.

You'll learn more about these and other LinkedIn features later in this book.

This chapter shows you how to create a quality profile that matches your LinkedIn goals.

2

Creating Your LinkedIn Profile

Profiles form the foundation of LinkedIn. Your profile is your LinkedIn calling card, providing a quick snapshot of your professional background and experience. Although creating a profile is a straightforward task, choosing the right profile content has a major impact on the success you achieve on LinkedIn.

In this chapter, you learn how to develop a profile strategy, create a quality profile, and extend your profile with supplemental content. You can also listen to tips on creating a profile that generates results and watch videos that show you how to create a basic profile, customize your public profile, and add a profile photo.

Exploring LinkedIn Profiles

Before creating your own profile, it's a good idea to view a variety of member profiles to get an idea of what makes a quality profile. Although you should focus on viewing the profiles of others in your field (in other words, a little "competitive intelligence"), also take the time to explore profiles of professionals in other fields and geographic regions.

Figure 2.1 illustrates a sample, completed LinkedIn profile.

A profile can include any of the following:

- A summary of your professional experience and specialties
- Your photo
- Your current status and a link to comments from your network
- A list of the positions you've held and your major accomplishments at each
- A list of the educational institutions you've attended and your major accomplishments at each
- Professional recommendations
- Data from LinkedIn applications, such as your blog feed, Amazon reading list, shared presentations, and more

- A list of your LinkedIn connections

- Information about your interests, association memberships, honors, and awards

- Your contact settings

- A list of your opportunity preferences

Figure 2.1 *A solid profile generates positive results on LinkedIn.*

Creating a Profile That Generates Results

Before you create your profile, you need to think strategically about what you want to accomplish. Here are some tips for creating a quality profile:

- Set goals for what you want to achieve on LinkedIn. Are you looking for a job? Do you want to develop your business and find new clients? Are you a recruiter seeking passive job candidates? Make sure that everything you include in your profile works toward achieving that goal.

- Make a list of keywords that relate to your experience, education, certifications, profession, and industry. Every industry has its buzzwords, and you need to include these if they're terms a recruiter or potential client would search for. For example, an IT professional may include keywords such as Java, Oracle, SAP, or AJAX. A project manager might select PMP, PMI, UML, SDLC, or Six Sigma. A public relations professional, on the other hand, could choose PRSA, APR, or social media.

- Have your current resume handy for easier profile completion. You can refer to it for any necessary dates or other data you might have forgotten.

If you really do want to include a resume on your LinkedIn profile, consider adding the Box.net Files application. With Box.net, you can share files such as PDF or Word documents on your profile. See Chapter 12, "Enhancing Your Profile with LinkedIn Applications," for more information about Box.net.

- Check for spelling and grammar errors. Nothing detracts more from a good profile than numerous typos.

- Remember that most people just scan your profile. You need to capture their attention quickly and not overwhelm them with unnecessary details that detract from your goals.

- Keep it professional. A few personal details such as your interests help humanize your profile, but too much emphasis on outside activities also detracts from your professional goals.

 TELL ME MORE   Media 2.1—Creating a LinkedIn Profile That **Generates Results**

Access this audio recording through your registered Web edition at **my.safaribooksonline.com/9780789745095/media.**

Keep privacy issues in mind as you complete your profile. Only enter data that you're willing to share publicly.

Achieving Profile Completeness

To view your profile completeness percentage, select Edit Profile from the Profile drop-down menu on the global navigation bar. The Edit My Profile page opens, shown in Figure 2.2.

On the right side of your screen, you'll see a box that displays your profile completeness. It should be about 25 percent at this point, just for signing up for a LinkedIn account. This box displays a list of the additional percentage points you receive for completing specific tasks.

You might notice that adding the listed percentages to your existing 25 percent still doesn't amount to 100 percent. That's because you need at least two past positions and three recommendations to achieve profile completeness.

Figure 2.2   *Create your profile on the Edit My Profile page.*

To achieve a profile completeness of 100 percent, you need to complete the following items:

- Your current position
- At least two past positions
- Your education
- A profile summary
- A profile photo
- Your specialties
- At least three recommendations

Having a complete profile encourages people to network with you. In fact, LinkedIn indicates that users with complete profiles are 40 times more likely to receive opportunities than those with incomplete profiles.

Just filling out the required fields to achieve 100-percent completion doesn't guarantee success. You also need the right profile content. A few words in a field may count toward a computer's view of "completeness," but it won't be effective if your profile still contains minimal information.

Creating a Basic Profile

Now that you have a plan for creating a solid profile, it's time to get started entering data.

SHOW ME   Media 2.2—Creating a Basic LinkedIn Profile
Access this video file through your registered Web edition at
my.safaribooksonline.com/9780789745095/media.

To add more content to the basic profile that LinkedIn creates when you sign up, select Edit Profile from the Profile drop-down menu on the global navigation bar.

The top portion of the Edit My Profile page (refer to Figure 2.2) displays your name, title, company, location, and industry based on the data you entered when you signed up. Click the Edit link next to any entry you want to change; this opens the Basic Information page.

The Post an Update link on the Edit My Profile page prompts you to share information with your LinkedIn connections. You can enter something now or wait until you have connections who actually view your status. See Chapter 5, "Maintaining Your LinkedIn Profile," for more information about updates.

The Basic Information page also includes several new fields. These include the following:

- **Former/Maiden Name**. If you've changed your name at any point during your career, it could be difficult for former classmates or colleagues to find you. Entering your former/maiden name makes it easier when people search for your former name.

- **Display Name**. By default, LinkedIn displays your full name. If you have strong privacy concerns, you can choose to display only your first name and last initial to anyone other than your own connections.

- **Professional Headline**. LinkedIn uses a combination of your title and company name as your professional headline, which should be sufficient for most people. You may want to customize this, however, if you're seeking work, are self-employed, or maintain more than one job. Some people include targeted keywords, professional certifications, or degrees in their professional headlines.

   Some examples are as follows:

   - PMP-Certified IT Project Manager Seeking New Opportunities

- Bestselling Author, Coach, and Business Consultant
- Public Relations Executive, MBA, APR, Fellow PRSA

Make your changes; then click the Save Changes button to return to the Edit My Profile page.

Adding Positions

Although you already entered your current job title and company when you created your LinkedIn account, you'll want to expand on that basic information. To do so, click the Edit link next to your current position on the Edit My Profile page to open the Edit Position page, shown in Figure 2.3.

Figure 2.3   *Let other LinkedIn members know about your professional success.*

If you already have a completed resume available in Microsoft Word, PDF, or HTML format, you can import it. LinkedIn scans your resume for experience and education information and suggests ways to map this data to your profile. To do so, click the Import Your Resume link on the right side of the screen. Although importing can save time, you might prefer to customize your LinkedIn profile by entering data manually.

Enter a brief description of your current position, make any additional changes to the information you previously entered, and click the Update button.

Here are a few tips on what to include in the Description field:

- **Use keywords.** Think of the terms people would search for and use them in your description. For example, if you work in IT, mention actual technologies rather than vague generalizations.

- **Emphasize accomplishments over job duties.** For example, rather than saying that you're responsible for sales, focus on your sales achievements and awards.

- **Be brief.** The Description field is a summary, not a detailed resume.

- **Keep your goals in mind.** If you want to attract recruiters, think about what would interest them in a potential candidate. If you're seeking clients for your business, focus on what would make them want to hire you.

Click the Remove This Position link at the bottom of the Edit Position page to delete that position from LinkedIn.

If you hold more than one current job, click the Add Current Position link on the Edit My Profile page to add another current position. This is particularly useful for self-employed or independent professionals who have several income sources. For example, if you're an author, consultant, and blogger, you could choose to combine these activities under one position or create a unique position for each activity.

Add past positions by clicking the Add Past Position link. Adding past positions is important because it provides a clearer view of your background and makes it easier to connect with your former colleagues at previous companies.

If you have extensive experience, it's a good idea to focus only on the past 10 to 15 years of your work life unless an early position in your career is very relevant to your current goals.

Adding Educational Information

Next, you'll add information about your educational background. LinkedIn uses this information to help you connect easily with former classmates.

Consider the following best practices when choosing what educational information to enter:

- Include colleges and universities from which you received a degree.

- Include *relevant* certificates and continuing education coursework. For example, if you're looking for a job in a new field and have completed a related certificate, you should include this information.

- Don't include every continuing education course or seminar you've ever taken. It's important to be strategic, not prolific.

- Don't include your high school information unless you're still in college, are a recent graduate, or specifically want to reconnect with high school classmates.

 LET ME TRY IT

Entering Educational Information

To enter educational information, follow these steps:

1. Click the Add Education link on the Edit My Profile page. The Add Education page opens, shown in Figure 2.4.

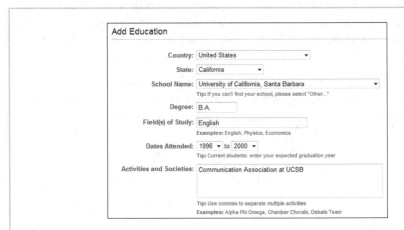

Figure 2.4 *Provide a summary of your educational accomplishments.*

2. Select your country. Depending on your country selection, LinkedIn might prompt you to enter additional information, such as a state or province.

3. Select your school name from the drop-down list that displays. If you can't find your school in the list, scroll down to the end and select Other. You can then enter your school name manually in the Type School Name field.

4. Enter your degree, such as BA, BS, or MBA.

5. Enter your field(s) of study. This can be your major, an area of concentration, or the name of a certificate.

6. In the Dates Attended fields, enter the years you attended. If you're still a student, enter your anticipated year of graduation in the second field.

The decision whether to include your year of graduation is a personal choice for many experienced professionals. LinkedIn doesn't require you to list the year you graduated; this is an optional field. Keep in mind, however, that LinkedIn won't be able to automatically search for your former classmates if you omit your graduation year. You would need to perform a manual search for former classmates.

7. List relevant activities in the Activities and Societies field. This might include honors, study abroad, and any extracurricular activities.

8. Add any additional notes about your educational experience.

9. Click the Save Changes button to return to the Edit My Profile page.

You don't need to complete all the fields on the Add Education page to provide an accurate picture of your educational background. For example, details about your participation with the ski club or theater groups might not add real value to your LinkedIn profile, particularly if you've been out of school for years and work in an unrelated field. Entering the most pertinent data ensures that people who read your profile focus on what's relevant.

The next section on the Edit My Profile page, Recommended, encourages you to request professional recommendations. My suggestion, however, is for you to first complete your profile and then add connections before requesting recommendations. See Chapter 10, "Managing LinkedIn Recommendations," for more information about LinkedIn recommendations.

Adding Websites and Other Information

Enhance your profile further by adding links to external websites as well as information about your interests, professional associations, honors, and awards.

To avoid clutter and prevent link spam, you can enter only three websites on your LinkedIn profile. If you have more than three sites, think carefully about which sites would generate the most interest on a business networking site such as LinkedIn.

LET ME TRY IT

Adding Website Links and Other Information to Your Profile

To list websites on your LinkedIn profile—as well as add other information about your interests and achievements—follow these steps:

1. On the Edit My Profile page, click the Add Websites link. The Additional Information page opens, shown in Figure 2.5.

Additional Information

Websites:	My Company ▾	http://www.pacificridgecon
	My Blog ▾	http://PRInsights.wordpres
	Choose... ▾	URL (ex: http://www.site.c

Interests:

Tip: Use commas to separate multiple interests
Examples: management training, new technology, investing, fishing, snowboarding... See more

Groups and Associations:

Tip: Use commas to separate multiple groups
Examples: Kiwanis, IEEE, Product Marketing Association... See more

Honors and Awards:

Figure 2.5   *Add links to your website or blog on your LinkedIn profile.*

2. From the Websites drop-down list, select the type of link you want to add. Options include: My Website, My Company, My Blog, My RSS Feed, My Portfolio, or Other. If you select Other, a text box appears in which you can enter the name of your choice.

> You can use the Other option to gain name recognition for your site or blog. For example, if you have a blog called Project Management Best Practices, you might prefer to create a link with that name rather than using the generic "My Website" or "My Blog."

3. Enter the complete URL of the site you want to link to, such as http://www.patricerutledge.com.

4. In the Interests text box, enter a list of your professional and personal interests. Be sure to use commas to separate interests so this content is searchable. Each interest becomes a link on your actual profile that you

can click to search for others who share your interests. Again, think about meaningful keywords for this section rather than lengthy descriptions.

5. List the groups and associations to which you belong. Use commas to separate this information as well because the terms also become searchable links on your profile.

6. List any honors and awards you've received.

7. Click the Save Changes button to update your profile and return to the Edit My Profile page.

Integrating Your LinkedIn Account with Twitter

If you have an account on Twitter (www.twitter.com), you might want to consider integrating it with LinkedIn. By doing so, you can share selected Twitter updates.

 LET ME TRY IT

Integrating LinkedIn and Twitter

To set up LinkedIn to integrate with Twitter, follow these steps:

1. On the Edit My Profile page, click the Add Twitter Account link.

2. In the pop-up box, enter your Twitter username or email as well as your password. If you're already logged in to Twitter, LinkedIn skips this step.

3. Click the Allow button.

4. In the next pop-up box (see Figure 2.6), specify whether you want to share all your tweets in your LinkedIn status or only selected tweets.

Figure 2.6 *Share your tweets on LinkedIn.*

In general, it's a good idea to be selective in sharing your tweets on LinkedIn. If you're a frequent Twitter user, some of your tweets might appear out of context on LinkedIn. To share only specific tweets, use the #in or #li hashtag at the end of any tweet you want to post as a LinkedIn status.

5. Click the Save Settings button.

To make changes to the way you integrate LinkedIn and Twitter, click the Edit link to the right of the Twitter field on the Edit My Profile page. On the Twitter Settings page, you can hide your Twitter username on your profile, change the way you share your tweets, remove Twitter integration, or add another Twitter account. See Chapter 4, "Customizing Your LinkedIn Experience," for more information about the Twitter Settings page.

You can also share your LinkedIn updates on Twitter by selecting the Twitter checkbox when you post updates. See Chapter 5 for more information. To further integrate your LinkedIn and Twitter accounts, consider adding the Tweets application to share your latest tweets on your profile and home page. See Chapter 12 for more information.

Customizing Public Profiles

LinkedIn makes a public version of your profile available to all Web users, regardless of whether they're LinkedIn members or connected to you. When someone searches your name on Google or Yahoo!, for example, the public version of your profile appears in search results. Although a public profile is a great way to promote your career and gain visibility, it isn't for everyone. Don't worry. You have control over exactly what others can view on your profile. You can even hide your profile from public view if you choose.

By default, your public LinkedIn URL looks something like this: http://www.linkedin.com/pub/patrice-anne-rutledge/13/521/845. The numbers in this URL address aren't very user-friendly, however, so you'll want to customize your public profile URL to something easier to remember, such as www.linkedin.com/in/patriceannerutledge.

 SHOW ME   **Media 2.3—Customizing Your Public Profile in LinkedIn**
Access this video file through your registered Web edition at
my.safaribooksonline.com/9780789745095/media.

 **LET ME TRY IT**

Customizing Your Public Profile

To customize your public profile, follow these steps:

1. On the Edit My Profile page, click the Customize Your URL link. The Public Profile page opens, as shown in Figure 2.7.

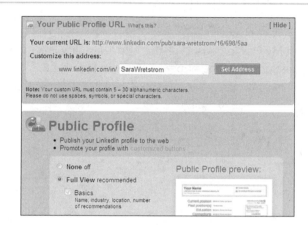

Figure 2.7   *Create a user-friendly URL for your LinkedIn public profile.*

2. Click the Edit link in the Your Public Profile URL section.

3. Enter the custom URL you prefer. Using your first name and last name as one string of characters is a good choice. Spaces, symbols, and special characters aren't allowed in your URL.

4. Click the Set Address button to save your changes.

5. In the Public Profile section, clear the check box next to any fields you do not want to appear on your public profile.

To hide your entire profile from public view on the Web, click the None option button in the Public Profile section.

6. Click the Save Changes button to update your public profile.

7. Click the View My Public Profile as Others See It link at the bottom of the page to preview what your public profile looks like on the Web.

Adding Profile Summaries

The next section on the Edit My Profile page asks you to enter a profile summary. This is an important step because people scanning your profile often read this section first.

 LET ME TRY IT

Adding Your Profile Summary

To create your summary, follow these steps:

1. On the Edit My Profile page, click the Add Summary link in the Summary section. The Summary page opens, shown in Figure 2.8.

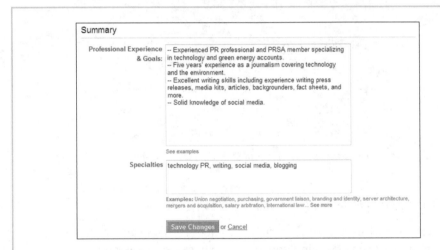

Figure 2.8   *Provide a concise summary of your professional accomplishments.*

To get some ideas about what to include in your summary section, analyze the profiles of others in your profession or industry. Each industry has its own buzzwords and "personality," so what works for one profession might not be as appropriate for another.

2. Enter a summary of your professional experience and goals. In addition to summarizing your professional experience, you can also use this field to indicate that you're looking for job opportunities (assuming you're currently unemployed), recruiting staff, accepting new clients, or seeking new business partners, for example. Be sure to keep it professional, however. This is not the place for an advertisement or sales hype.

3. List your professional specialties in the Specialties field. You can use this area to enter additional keywords or to expand on your experience.

4. Click the Save Changes button to return to the Edit My Profile page.

The next section on the Edit My Profile page, Applications, suggests several applications you can add to your profile. See Chapter 12 for more information about the many ways you can benefit from LinkedIn applications.

The next four sections—Experience, Education, Recommended By, and Additional Information—appeared earlier on the Edit My Profile page. You can click the Edit link in any of these sections to make additional changes, or you can continue to the next section.

Adding Personal Information

At the bottom of the Edit My Profile page, you'll find the Personal Information section. In this section, you can enter the following data:

- Phone
- Address
- IM (instant message)
- Birthday
- Marital Status

If you want to add any of this information to your profile, click the Edit link to open the Personal Information page. The Birthday, Birth Year, and Marital Status fields display a lock button next to them. Click this button to restrict visibility to only your connections or only your network.

Entering any data in the Personal Information section is optional. Carefully consider your personal privacy before making any personal information public, even to a restricted group of people.

Specifying Contact Settings

Next, specify what types of messages you'll accept and what opportunities you're interested in.

LET ME TRY IT

Specifying Your Contact Settings

To update the Contact Settings page, shown in Figure 2.9, follow these steps:

1. At the bottom of the Edit My Profile page, click the Edit link next to the Contact Settings heading.

2. In the What Type Of Messages Will You Accept? field, indicate whether you'll accept both introductions and InMail or if you'll accept only introductions. See Chapter 6, "Communicating with Your LinkedIn Network," for more information about InMail and introductions.

3. In the Opportunity Preferences section, indicate the opportunities you're open to. If you're looking for a job or recruiting staff, for example, it's important to let people know this. Your options include the following:

   - Career opportunities
   - Expertise requests
   - Consulting offers
   - Business deals
   - New ventures
   - Personal reference requests
   - Job inquiries
   - Requests to reconnect

Contact Settings

Besides helping you find people and opportunities through your network, LinkedIn makes it easy for opportunities to find you. In deciding how other LinkedIn users may contact you, take care not to exclude contacts inadvertently that you might find professionally valuable.

What type of messages will you accept?

- ⦿ I'll accept Introductions and InMail
- ◯ I'll accept only Introductions

Opportunity Preferences

What kinds of opportunities would you like to receive?

- ☑ Career opportunities   ☑ Expertise requests
- ☑ Consulting offers   ☑ Business deals
- ☑ New ventures   ☑ Personal reference requests
- ☑ Job inquiries   ☑ Requests to reconnect

What advice would you give to users considering contacting you?

Include comments on your availability, types of projects or opportunities that interest you, and what information you'd like to see included in a request. To avoid unwanted contacts, do not include contact information, since your response will be visible to your entire network. See examples.

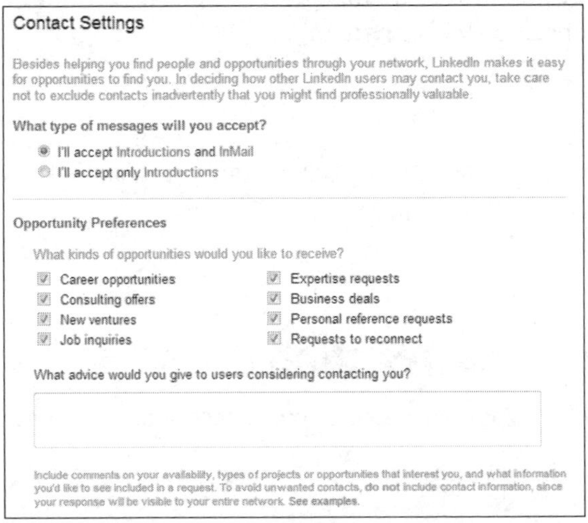

Figure 2.9 *Tell other LinkedIn members about your contact preferences.*

4. Enter the advice you would give to members considering contacting you. In this text box, you can indicate that you're open to connecting with new people, you want to connect only with people you know, and so forth.

5. Click the Save Changes button to return to the Edit My Profile page.

Adding Profile Photos

Finally, you should add a photo to your LinkedIn profile. A photo helps bring your profile to life and sets you apart from other LinkedIn members. A professional headshot works best on your LinkedIn profile.

 SHOW ME   Media 2.4—Adding Your Profile Photo
Access this video file through your registered Web edition at
my.safaribooksonline.com/9780789745095/media.

 LET ME TRY IT

Adding Your Profile Photo

To upload your photo, follow these steps:

1. At the top of the Edit My Profile page, click the Add Photo link. Figure 2.10 shows the page that appears.

Figure 2.10   *Let a professional photo bring your LinkedIn profile to life.*

2. Click the Browse button to open the Choose File to Upload dialog box.

3. Select the photo you want to upload and click the Open button. Depending on your operating system, the name of this button could vary.

You can upload a photo in a JPG, GIF, or PNG file format, and the file cannot be larger than 4 MB.

4. Click the Upload Photo button. LinkedIn shows you a preview of how your photo will appear on your profile.

5. Use LinkedIn's resizing tool to make any modifications and click the Save Photo button to complete the upload process.

6. Indicate your photo visibility preferences. You can specify that your photo is visible to your connections, to your network, or to everyone. Note that your connections include only the people you directly connect with; your network includes the people connected to your connections.

7. Click the Save Settings button to finish the upload and return to the Edit My Profile page.

If you want to replace or remove your profile photo, click the Edit link below your photo on the Edit My Profile page. Here you can upload a new photo or click the Delete Photo link to remove your photo.

Reordering Sections on Your LinkedIn Profile

LinkedIn displays the sections on your profile in an order that works well for most people, but you can change this if you like. On the Edit My Profile page, click the handle that appears to the left of each section (such as Summary, Experience, Education, and so on), and drag that section to a new location on your profile. This way, you can highlight the profile content you want other members to see first.

Viewing Your Profile

To preview your profile, select View Profile from the Profile drop-down menu on the global navigation bar. Alternatively, click the View My Profile tab if you're currently on the Edit My Profile page.

Review all your entries carefully, checking for content accuracy as well as for grammar and spelling errors. If necessary, revise any of your entries by clicking the Edit link next to the item you want to edit.

See Chapter 5, "Maintaining Your LinkedIn Profile," for more information about keeping your profile updated, printing your profile, promoting your profile on the Web, and creating a profile in another language.

This chapter shows you how to develop a solid
LinkedIn network that achieves your networking
goals.

3

Developing Your LinkedIn Network

After creating a strong profile, the next step in making the most of your LinkedIn experience is developing a solid network of professional connections. Before you add connections to LinkedIn, however, you should develop a connection strategy that matches your goals and networking philosophy.

In this chapter, you explore the many ways to build and manage your LinkedIn network. You can also listen to advice on developing a connection strategy and watch videos that show you how to import your webmail contacts, connect with people not on LinkedIn, and respond to connection invitations.

Developing a Connection Strategy

There is no one "right" way to develop your LinkedIn network. All LinkedIn members are unique and need to follow a personalized strategy that focuses on their own goals, industry, position, and comfort level with networking.

 TELL ME MORE   Media 3.1—Developing Your LinkedIn Connection Strategy

Access this audio recording through your registered Web Edition at my.safaribooksonline.com/9780789745095/media.

The three most common approaches are as follows:

- **Connect only with people you know.** LinkedIn members who follow this approach connect only with colleagues, classmates, and associates they personally know or who their known connections recommend to them.

- **Connect with anyone and everyone.** Some LinkedIn members, particularly those who want to use the site for business development purposes, are open networkers and like to connect with as many people as possible and make special efforts to connect with thousands of people.

- **Connect with people you know, plus strategic contacts you would like to know.** With this approach, you connect with people you know and also seek out strategic connections who match your networking goals.

Which approach is best? There is no one right answer for everyone. LinkedIn members have their own goals as to what they hope to accomplish on the site, as well as their own networking strategies and comfort levels.

To get started, here's a list of some people you may want to connect with:

- Current and former colleagues

- Current and former classmates

- Friends and other acquaintances

- Fellow members of professional associations

Who to connect with beyond these obvious contacts depends on your connection strategy and networking philosophy.

Building Your Network

When you first join LinkedIn, your home page displays the Build Your Network box, shown in Figure 3.1.

Figure 3.1   *Building a solid network of contacts is a critical step in making the most of LinkedIn's potential.*

This box encourages you to import your webmail contacts and search for people you know who are already on LinkedIn. You can also import your contacts from desktop email programs such as Microsoft Outlook or Apple Mail from the Build Your Network box.

Importing your webmail or desktop email contacts doesn't mean these people automatically become LinkedIn connections. You still have the flexibility to manually choose whom to connect with.

After you create a profile and develop a network of more than 20 connections, LinkedIn enables you to close the Build Your Network box by clicking the Close (x) button that appears in the upper-right corner.

Importing Webmail Contacts

If you have an email account with a popular webmail provider (such as Windows Live Hotmail, Gmail, Yahoo! Mail, or AOL), LinkedIn can import the email addresses of your Web contacts.

 SHOW ME   Media 3.2—Importing Your Webmail Contacts in LinkedIn
Access this video file through your registered Web Edition at
my.safaribooksonline.com/9780789745095/media.

 LET ME TRY IT

Importing Your Webmail Contacts

To import webmail contacts, follow these steps:

1. In the Build Your Network box, enter your email and password for a specific webmail account. Click the Learn More link for a complete list of webmail providers that LinkedIn supports.

You can also import webmail contacts by clicking the Add Connections link above the global navigation bar and then entering your email address and password in the See Who You Already Know on LinkedIn box.

2. Click the Continue button. The Add Connections page opens, listing potential contacts for you to invite (see Figure 3.2).

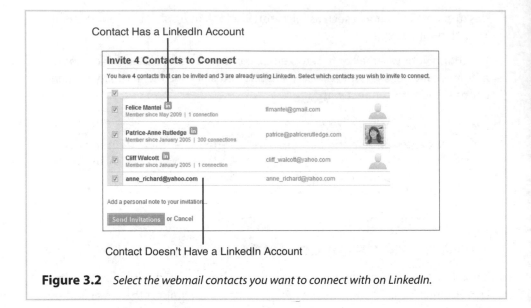

Contact Has a LinkedIn Account

Contact Doesn't Have a LinkedIn Account

Figure 3.2 *Select the webmail contacts you want to connect with on LinkedIn.*

3. By default, LinkedIn includes a checkmark next to every name on your list. If there's someone you don't want to connect with on LinkedIn, remove the checkmark next to that person's name.

4. Click the Send Invitations button to send your LinkedIn invitations.

Your contacts will receive your connection requests and choose to accept or reject your request. If you want to import webmail contacts from another webmail account, repeat these steps using your email address and password for that webmail provider.

If you don't send an invitation to every match from your webmail accounts right away, you can do so later. On the global navigation bar, select Imported Contacts from the Contacts drop-down menu to view a list of your email contacts you aren't already connected to on LinkedIn (see Figure 3.3). You can invite any of these people from this page.

You can't send connection requests until you confirm your email address. If you need to request a new confirmation message from LinkedIn, click the Settings link in the global navigation bar and then click the Email Addresses link. Select the email address you want to confirm and click the Send Confirmation Message button. LinkedIn sends you an email with confirmation instructions.

Figure 3.3   *View a list of imported email contacts.*

Importing Contacts from Desktop Email Programs

In addition to importing webmail contacts, you can also import contacts from desktop email programs such as Microsoft Outlook or Apple Mail.

Although LinkedIn imports webmail contacts automatically, you need to export your contacts from desktop programs as a separate step. To do so, follow the instructions your email system provides for exporting your email address book data to one of the following:

- A comma-separated values (CSV) file, which is a computer file in which fields are separated by commas with a .CSV filename extension.

- A vCard file, which is a file format for electronic business cards with a .VCF filename extension.

- A tab-separated file, which is a computer file in which fields are separated by tabs with a .TXT filename extension.

LinkedIn accepts the following files for import:

- CSV files from Microsoft Outlook

- CSV or tab-separated files from Palm Desktop

- CSV files from ACT!

- vCard files from Palm Desktop

- vCard files from Mac OS X Address Book

 **LET ME TRY IT**

Importing Your Contacts from Desktop Email Programs

To import a file exported from an email program, follow these steps:

1. In the Build Your Network box, click the Import Desktop Email Contacts link.

> You can also import email contacts by clicking the Add Connections link on the global navigation bar and then clicking the Import Your Desktop Email Contacts link.

2. Click the Browse button to select the appropriate file on your computer.

3. Click the Upload File button. LinkedIn imports your file and opens the Add Connections page, listing potential contacts for you to invite (refer to Figure 3.2).

4. By default, LinkedIn includes a checkmark next to every name on your list. If there's someone you don't want to connect with on LinkedIn, remove the checkmark next to that person's name.

5. Click the Send Invitations button to send your LinkedIn invitations.

Your contacts will receive your connection requests and choose to accept or reject your request.

If you don't send an invitation to every match right away, you can do so later. On the global navigation bar, select Imported Contacts from the Contacts drop-down menu to view a list of your email contacts you already aren't connected to on LinkedIn (refer to Figure 3.3). You can invite any of these people from this page.

Connecting with Colleagues

Connecting with the people you work with—or worked with in the past—is one of the best ways of expanding your LinkedIn network. If you imported contacts from your mail system, you might have already connected with many of your colleagues. In addition, you can also search for colleagues who aren't in your email address book.

LET ME TRY IT

Finding and Connecting with Your Colleagues

To connect with current or past colleagues, follow these steps:

1. Click the Add Connections link above the global navigation bar to open the Add Connections page.

2. Click the Colleagues tab. Figure 3.4 shows the page that appears.

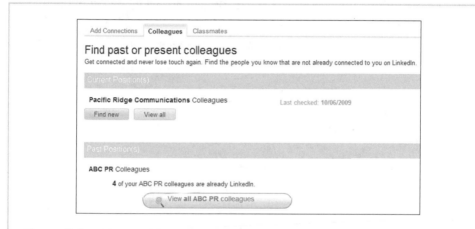

Figure 3.4   *Connecting with your current and past colleagues is a great way to build your online network.*

3. For your current employer, click the View All button if you're searching for colleagues for the first time. If you want to search for colleagues new to LinkedIn, click the Find New button. Alternatively, click the View All [Company Name] Colleagues for any past employers. The Invite Colleagues page opens, which displays a list of colleagues who worked at this company at the same time as you.

4. Select the individuals you know.

5. Click the Send Invitations button to send connection requests to these people.

Select the Add a Personal Note with Your Invitation? check box to add a personalized greeting to your connection request. Personalizing your request is particularly useful when reaching out to colleagues you haven't worked with in a while.

Connecting with Classmates

Connecting with current or former classmates is another smart LinkedIn connection strategy.

 LET ME TRY IT

Connecting with Your Classmates

To connect with classmates, follow these steps:

1. Click the Add Connections link above the global navigation bar to open the Add Connections page.

2. Click the Classmates tab. Figure 3.5 shows the page that appears.

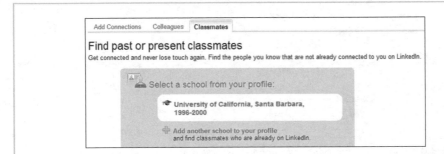

Figure 3.5 *Connecting with classmates is another good way to develop your LinkedIn network.*

3. Click the button for the school you want to search. LinkedIn provides buttons for any current or former schools you include on your profile. The Classmates/Search Results page opens, which displays a list of classmates who attended this school at the same time as you.

4. View the search results and click the Invite link for the classmates you want to connect with. You can narrow or widen your search results by selecting View Graduation Year Only or View All Years Attended.

If you didn't finish adding schools to your profile, click the Add Another School to Your Profile link to find classmates from additional schools.

Connecting with Others on LinkedIn

By now, you should have a good start on developing your LinkedIn network. Here are a few other suggestions for finding worthwhile connections on LinkedIn:

- Review the list of people your connections are connected to, which displays in their profile. It's very likely that you know some of the same people and would like to connect with them as well. View the profile of the person you want to connect with and click the Add [person's name] to Your Network link to send an invitation from the Add Connections page. For example, to connect with Emily Adamson, you would click the Add Emily to Your Network link.

- Search for individuals by name in the search box on the global navigation bar. Click the Add to Network link to the right of the person you want to connect with to open the Add Connections page. For additional search options, click the Advanced link.

- Search by keyword and location on the Advanced Search page to find local members of your professional associations. Click the Advanced link on the global navigation bar to access this page. For example, you could search for the keyword PRSA (for the Public Relations Society of America) and the zip code 92606 within a 25-mile radius to find fellow PRSA members in Orange County, California.

- Search for potential connections among the members of any LinkedIn groups to which you belong. The Members tab (available from the More drop-down list) provides a list of all group members and an Invite to Connect link with which to contact them. Remember, however, not to spam fellow group members with connection invitations. Be selective in determining who you want to connect with.

See Chapter 7, "Searching for People on LinkedIn," for more information on searching for people.

When you click the Add to Network link from any of these options, the Add Connections page appears, shown in Figure 3.6.

 LET ME TRY IT

Connecting with Other LinkedIn Members

To create a connection request on this page, follow these steps:

1. Select how you know your target connection from these options:
   - **Colleague.** Select a company from the drop-down list that appears.

- **Classmate.** Select a school from the drop-down list that appears.
- **We've Done Business Together.** Select a company from the drop-down list that appears.
- **Friend.**
- **Groups.** Select a group from the drop-down list that appears.
- **Other.** Enter the person's email address.
- **I Don't Know [person's name].**

Figure 3.6 *Specify how you know a target connection before sending an invitation.*

If you haven't completed your profile data, you may see only a text box to enter your target connection's email address on this page.

2. Include a personal note in the text box explaining why you want to connect on LinkedIn. This is particularly important if you don't know the person you want to connect with.

3. Click the Send Invitation button to send your connection request.

See Chapter 6, "Communicating with Your LinkedIn Network," for more information on viewing the status of connection invitations and other messages.

Two other ways of connecting with people you don't know are to send an InMail or request an introduction. See Chapter 6 for more information on InMail and introductions.

Connecting with People Not on LinkedIn

If you discover that some of your real-world networking contacts aren't using LinkedIn yet, it's easy to invite them.

 SHOW ME   Media 3.3—Connecting with People Not on LinkedIn
Access this video file through your registered Web Edition at
my.safaribooksonline.com/9780789745095/media.

 LET ME TRY IT

Connecting with Your Colleagues Not on LinkedIn

To send a connection invitation to someone who doesn't have a LinkedIn account, follow these steps:

1. Click the Add Connections link above the global navigation bar to open the Add Connections page.

2. In the Enter Email Address box (see Figure 3.7), enter the email address of the person or persons you want to invite. Separate multiple addresses with a comma.

Figure 3.7   *Invite your real-world connections to join LinkedIn.*

3. Click the Send Invitations button to send invitations.

Your contacts receive an email from LinkedIn letting them know you want to connect with them.

Responding to Connection Invitations

In addition to sending invitations to connect, you might also receive invitations. LinkedIn lets you decide whether or not to accept the invitation. You can also ask senders for more information, such as the reason they want to connect (if you don't know them or there is no obvious professional link).

 SHOW ME   Media 3.4—Responding to LinkedIn Connection Invitations
Access this video file through your registered Web Edition at
my.safaribooksonline.com/9780789745095/media.

 **LET ME TRY IT**

Responding to Your Connection Invitations

To respond to an invitation, follow these steps:

1. Click the Inbox link on the global navigation bar to open your Inbox. If you have new messages, LinkedIn displays the number of messages in parentheses, such as Inbox (2).

2. If you have a lot of messages in your Inbox, click the Invitations link below the search box. Your Inbox displays only your invitation requests. Alternatively, you can also view new invitation requests in your Inbox preview on your home page.

> If you specified that you want to receive invitations to connect by email on the Settings page, your invitations also arrive by email. Click the link in the email to open the Invitations page.

3. To open the request, click the Subject Line link. Figure 3.8 illustrates a sample request to connect.

4. View the greeting from the person who wants to connect with you.

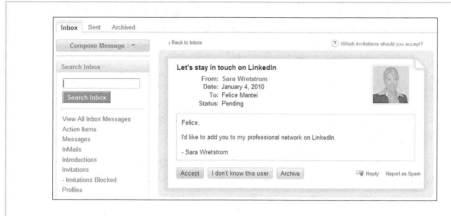

Figure 3.8   *You must manually accept invitations to connect.*

5. If you would like to open the individual's profile, click the sender's name. Reviewing a LinkedIn member's profile can help you remember more about someone you don't know well or decide whether to connect with someone you don't know at all.

6. Take one of the following actions:
    - If you want to add the person to your network, click the Accept button.
    - If you want to decline the invitation, click the I Don't Know This User button. LinkedIn blocks this person from inviting you again, but you can send an invitation if you decide to do so in the future. Be aware that receiving too many "I don't know" responses penalizes senders and could block their ability to connect with others. It's best to use this response for connection invitations you consider "spam" as opposed to genuine requests from people you would prefer just not to connect with.
    - If you don't have time to review the invitation, click the Archive button to move the invitation to your Archived folder. You can accept or decline the invitation in the future.
    - To send a message to the person who initiated the invitation before accepting or declining, click the Reply link. For example, you might want to ask why this person wants to connect before accepting.
    - If you feel this invitation is spam, click the Report as Spam link.

Be sure that an invitation truly is spam before reporting it. Reporting an invitation as spam is too harsh if it's a genuine request from someone you just don't want to connect with. Reporting as spam is appropriate, however, if the personalized greeting contains an overt sales pitch rather than a true connection invitation.

When you accept invitations, LinkedIn adds those members as 1st degree connections in your network. If you would like to add notes about these people and edit their contact information, use the Notes box on their profile.

Managing Your Connections

Once you develop your LinkedIn network, you need an easy way to find and manage your existing connections. The My Connections page offers several ways to do this.

Click the Contacts link on the global navigation bar to open the My Connections page, which displays a list of your connections (see Figure 3.9).

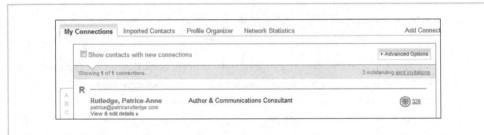

Figure 3.9   *Find, contact, and manage your connections on the My Connections page.*

If you have many connections, it may be difficult to find the person you're looking for. LinkedIn offers several ways to filter your connections. You can

- Click the first letter of a contact's last name to display only those contacts whose names start with that letter. If you don't have any contacts for a specific letter, that letter's link isn't displayed.

- Select the Show Contacts with New Connections check box. Doing this lets you know which of your contacts recently connected with someone new on LinkedIn. Perhaps you know this person and would like to connect as well?

- Click the Advanced Options button to filter by Location or Industry.

The View & Edit Details link beneath each connection's name opens a window where you can enter more detailed information about this connection, such as a phone number or website URL. To view a connection's profile, click on that individual's name.

If you're part of the Connections beta, you might view a different version of the My Connections page. This beta version offers advanced connection tagging and filtering for easier connection management.

Removing Connections

If you decide that you no longer want to connect with someone on LinkedIn, you can remove that person as a connection.

  LET ME TRY IT

Removing Unwanted Connections

To remove someone as a connection, follow these steps:

1. Click the Contacts link on the global navigation bar to open the My Connections page.

2. Click the Remove Connections link in the upper-right corner of the page.

3. Select the check box next to the connections you want to remove.

4. Click the Remove Connections button.

People you remove are no longer able to view any data that can be viewed only by actual connections, and they also can't send you direct messages. LinkedIn, however, doesn't notify them of the fact that they have been removed.

Be sure that a connection really warrants removal before proceeding with the removal process. For example, if a connection you don't know well is bothering you with requests, spam, or sales pitches, this person is probably a connection worth removing. Removing former colleagues or associates simply because you haven't seen them in a while or don't work with them anymore, however, can be shortsighted.

Exporting Connections

You can export your LinkedIn connections to archive for safekeeping or import into a mail program. LinkedIn enables you to export your connection data to any of the following formats:

- Microsoft Outlook .CSV file

- Outlook Express .CSV file

- Yahoo! Mail .CSV file

- Mac OS X Address Book .VCF file

- vCard .VCF file

 **LET ME TRY IT**

Exporting Your Connections

To export your LinkedIn connections, follow these steps:

1. Click the Contacts link on the global navigation bar to open the My Connections page.

2. Click the Export Connections link at the bottom of the page. The Export LinkedIn Connections page opens, shown in Figure 3.10.

3. Select the format you want from the Export To drop-down list.

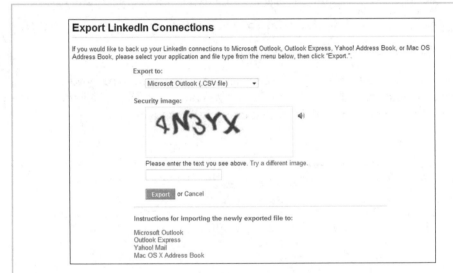

Figure 3.10 *Export your connections for safekeeping or to import into another email program.*

4. Enter the text that appears in the security image.

5. Click the Export button.

Links to instructions for importing your LinkedIn connections appear at the bottom of the page.

Viewing Your Network Statistics

The Network Statistics page, shown in Figure 3.11, provides some interesting statistics about your network of connections.

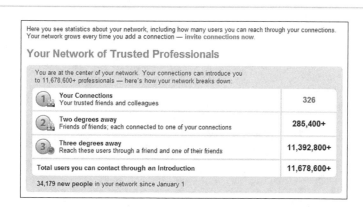

Here you see statistics about your network, including how many users you can reach through your connections. Your network grows every time you add a connection — invite connections now.

Your Network of Trusted Professionals

You are at the center of your network. Your connections can introduce you to 11,678,600+ professionals — here's how your network breaks down:

1	**Your Connections** Your trusted friends and colleagues	326
2	**Two degrees away** Friends of friends; each connected to one of your connections	285,400+
3	**Three degrees away** Reach these users through a friend and one of their friends	11,392,800+
	Total users you can contact through an Introduction	11,678,600+

34,179 new people in your network since January 1

Figure 3.11   *Analyze your LinkedIn network for insightful information and trends.*

To view these stats, select Network Statistics from the Contacts drop-down menu on the global navigation bar. On this page, you can view the following:

- Your total number of connections

- The number of connections who are two or three degrees away

- The number of members you can reach through an introduction

- The number of new people in your network over the past few days

- Your percentage of connections by geographic location and industry

To many people, these statistics might seem interesting but not particularly useful. If you're using LinkedIn as a business development tool, however, this insight might be more meaningful.

This chapter teaches you how to customize your
LinkedIn profile, email, and privacy settings.

4

Customizing Your LinkedIn Experience

Now that you've created a profile and connected with other LinkedIn members, it's time to customize your LinkedIn settings to optimize your experience on the site. If you're not sure which options to choose, selecting the ones that provide you with the most privacy and simplicity while still enabling you to achieve your goals is a good start.

In this chapter, you explore the many options on the Account & Settings page that enable you to personalize the way you use LinkedIn. You can also listen to customization tips and watch videos that show you how to customize email notification settings, personalize your home page, and subscribe to LinkedIn data through RSS feeds.

Customizing LinkedIn on the Account & Settings Page

The Account & Settings page provides a lengthy list of options for customizing your LinkedIn experience. To access this page, shown in Figure 4.1, click the Settings link above the global navigation bar.

The top portion of the Account & Settings page describes options for upgrading your account. See Chapter 1, "Introducing LinkedIn," to learn more about LinkedIn account options and upgrades.

 TELL ME MORE   Media 4.1—Customizing LinkedIn on the Account & Settings Page

Access this audio recording through your registered Web edition at **my.safaribooksonline.com/9780789745095/media.**

The many options provided on the Account & Settings page might seem over-whelming at first, and you might be tempted to skip this step. Setting aside some time to customize the options on this page, which is often a one-time task, can pay off in the long run. By customizing your LinkedIn settings, you'll better protect your privacy, receive only the specific information you want, and avoid any unpleasant surprises regarding the way LinkedIn handles your personal data.

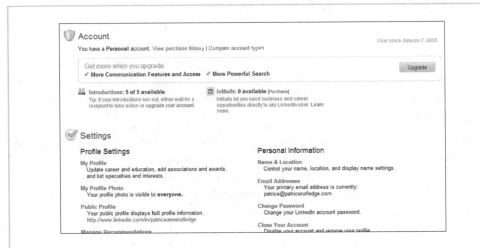

Figure 4.1 *The Account & Settings page provides numerous options for customizing your LinkedIn experience.*

Customizing Profile Settings

To customize your profile settings, click the Settings link above the global naviga-tion bar. In the Profile Settings section of this page, you can customize the following:

- **My Profile.** Update and edit your profile content on the Edit Profile page.

- **My Profile Photo.** Upload or remove your profile photo. If you don't want everyone to view your photo, you can restrict its visibility to only your net-work or only your connections.

Several of the options on this page give you the option to restrict visibility to My Connections or to My Network. My Connections refers to the LinkedIn members you connect with directly. My Network refers to the people two or three degrees away from your connections (in other words, your connections' connections). See Chapter 6, "Communicating with Your LinkedIn Network," for more informa-tion about this distinction.

- **Public Profile.** Specify the content you want to include in your public profile and customize your Web URL.

- **Manage Recommendations.** Request, provide, and manage recommendations. See Chapter 10, "Managing LinkedIn Recommendations," for more information about the power of LinkedIn recommendations.

- **Member Feed Visibility.** Your member feed refers to the network updates that appear on your home page and the home page of your connections. Make your member feed visible to everyone or restrict it to your network or connections. For maximum privacy, you can choose to not display your member feed.

- **Twitter Settings.** Enable your LinkedIn account to integrate with Twitter. If you've already added your Twitter account, you can change your access settings or disable the integration at any time. See Chapter 2, "Creating Your LinkedIn Profile," for more information about integrating LinkedIn and Twitter.

Customizing Email Notification Settings

LinkedIn enables you to make extensive customizations to the way you handle email notification of various actions and activities. To customize your email notification settings, click the Settings link above the global navigation bar.

 SHOW ME   Media 4.2—Customizing Email Notification Settings in LinkedIn

Access this video file through your registered Web edition at my.safaribooksonline.com/9780789745095/media.

The Email Notifications section of the Account & Settings page offers three customization options:

- Your contact settings

- The way you receive messages

- The invitations you receive

To customize your contact settings, such as the way you handle InMail and introductions, click the Contact Settings link. See Chapter 2 for more information about contact settings.

To customize how you receive messages on LinkedIn, click the Receiving Messages link. The Receiving Messages page appears, shown in Figure 4.2.

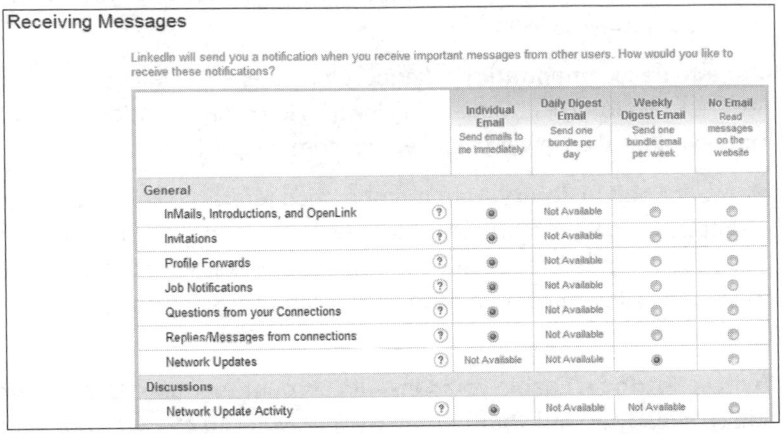

Receiving Messages

LinkedIn will send you a notification when you receive important messages from other users. How would you like to receive these notifications?

		Individual Email Send emails to me immediately	Daily Digest Email Send one bundle per day	Weekly Digest Email Send one bundle email per week	No Email Read messages on the website
General					
InMails, Introductions, and OpenLink	(?)	◉	Not Available	○	○
Invitations	(?)	◉	Not Available	○	○
Profile Forwards	(?)	◉	Not Available	○	○
Job Notifications	(?)	◉	Not Available	○	○
Questions from your Connections	(?)	◉	Not Available	○	○
Replies/Messages from connections	(?)	◉	Not Available	○	○
Network Updates	(?)	Not Available	Not Available	◉	○
Discussions					
Network Update Activity	(?)	◉	Not Available	Not Available	○

Figure 4.2   *LinkedIn enables you to provide specific instructions on its delivery of email messages.*

You have four choices on the way you receive messages:

- **Individual Email.** LinkedIn sends an email to your primary email address as soon as the action takes place.

- **Daily Digest Email.** LinkedIn sends one bundled email notification per day.

- **Weekly Digest Email.** LinkedIn sends one bundled email notification per week.

- **No Email.** LinkedIn sends no email. You need to go to the website to read messages and notifications.

With bundled notifications, you don't receive a notification if there is no activity.

You can further customize your notifications based on the type of message:

- InMails, introductions, and OpenLink messages from members outside your network

- Invitations to connect

- Profile forwards from your connections

- Job notification forwards from your connections

- Questions from your connections

- Replies and messages from your connections

- Network updates about your connections' LinkedIn activities

- Discussion update activity

- Invitations to join groups

- Group digest email by individual group

As you expand your network on LinkedIn, you could potentially receive a large volume of messages. Think carefully about how you best manage and process information. Many choose to receive email notifications of the updates that are most important to them and review online those that are less time-sensitive. For example, you might want to receive connection invitations and job notifications immediately, but review group news only on the Web. If you decide that your choices aren't working well for you, you can always modify these selections.

Not all notification methods are available for each type of message. For example, daily digest emails are available only for group notifications. Additionally, you can't receive network updates by individual email as this would involve more messages than most members want to handle.

Finally, you can customize which connection invitations you receive by clicking the Invitation Filtering link on the Account & Settings page. By default, you receive all invitations, but you can choose to receive invitations only from those who know your email address or those who are in your Imported Contacts list. Keep in mind, however, that restricting your invitations could block an invitation from someone you might actually want to connect with.

Customizing Home Page Settings

Network updates on your home page give you a quick snapshot of your connections' activities on LinkedIn. Although it's good to keep up with the latest news in your network, you might find that some network updates are of more interest to you than others are.

See Chapter 1 for more information about your home page.

Fortunately, there's a way to customize exactly what appears on your home page. You can choose which of the following updates you want to view and which you want to hide:

- New network connections

- Your connections' updates

- Your connections' profile updates, including content, photo, and recommendation updates

- Questions and answers from your connections

- Jobs posted by your connections

- Events your connections are hosting or attending

- Polls from your connections

- Group updates, including groups your connections have joined

- Application updates from your connections

- Company profile updates

 SHOW ME   Media 4.3—Customizing Your Home Page Settings in LinkedIn
Access this video file through your registered Web edition at
my.safaribooksonline.com/9780789745095/media.

 LET ME TRY IT

Customizing Your Home Page Settings

To customize your home page settings:

1. Click the Settings link above the global navigation bar.

2. On the Account & Settings page, click the Network Updates link in the Home Page Settings section.

3. Click the Manage Updates by Type tab, shown in Figure 4.3.

4. Specify how many updates you want to view on your home page. The default is 15, but you can choose from 10 to 25 updates.

5. Specify whether you want to Show or Hide each of the identified updates.

		Show Show on your home page	Hide Hide on your home page
Manage Updates by Connection | **Manage Updates by Type**			
Show or hide updates			
Control how many updates you would like to see on your homepage and which types you would like to see. How many updates would you like to see on your homepage? 15 ▾			
General			
	New connections in your network	◉	○
	Changes to your connections' status	◉	○
Profile & Recommendations			
	When connections change profile information	◉	○
	When connections change profile photos	◉	○
	When connections receive recommendations	◉	○
	When connections upgrade to a premium account	◉	○
Questions & Answers			
	Questions from your connections	◉	○
	Answers from your connections	◉	○

Figure 4.3   *Customize the content that appears on your home page.*

6. Click the Save Changes button. LinkedIn immediately makes the specified changes to your home page.

Subscribing to RSS Feeds

If you use a feed reader such as My Yahoo!, Google Reader, Newsgator, Bloglines, or Netvibes to subscribe to and read your favorite blog and news feeds, you might be interested in adding several LinkedIn RSS feeds.

SHOW ME   Media 4.4—Subscribing to RSS Feeds in LinkedIn
Access this video file through your registered Web edition at
my.safaribooksonline.com/9780789745095/media.

RSS stands for Really Simple Syndication, a popular format for Web feeds. Content publishers can syndicate their content with a feed, making it available for users to subscribe to it and view with feed reader applications. Feeds for blog content are most common, but you can also create a feed for Web content such as the content on LinkedIn. The advantage of feeds for the user is that you can view frequently updated content from your favorite blogs, podcasts, news sites, and other websites in one place. The standard feed icon is a small orange square with white radio waves, letting you know that the content is available via feed for your subscription.

To subscribe to LinkedIn feeds, click the Settings link above the global navigation bar. On the Account & Settings page, click the Your Private RSS Feeds link in the RSS Settings section. Figure 4.4 shows the page that opens.

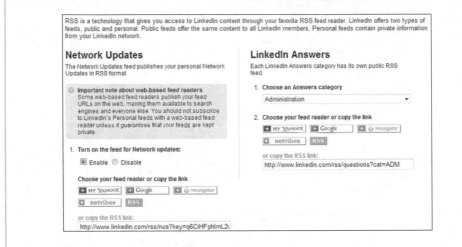

Figure 4.4   *You can view LinkedIn content with your favorite feed reader.*

Subscribing to Network Updates

LinkedIn offers a private RSS feed of the network updates that appear on your home page. It's important to understand the difference between a private feed and a public feed. LinkedIn private feeds contain personal data such as your updates and your connections' updates and are meant for your private viewing. Public feeds contain data available for public viewing, such as LinkedIn content that any member can access.

To subscribe to this feed, select the Enable option button and choose your favorite feed reader from the buttons that appear. You can also copy the RSS link and use it in another feed reader if you prefer.

Be careful not to publish your private feed on the Web. If you use a web-based feed reader, verify that your data will remain private if you don't want others to view your LinkedIn network updates.

Subscribing to LinkedIn Answers

You can also subscribe to a public feed of your favorite LinkedIn Answers categories. As you recall, a public feed contains data that's available to all LinkedIn users. Each LinkedIn Answers category maintains its own feed, so you can subscribe to one or more feeds based on your personal interests.

To subscribe, select a category from the drop-down list and click the button for your preferred feed reader. You can also copy the RSS link to use it in another feed reader.

LinkedIn also offers a public RSS feed for LinkedIn news updates. To access this feed, go to http://learn.linkedin.com/whats-new/ and click the orange RSS feed icon to subscribe with your favorite feed reader.

Customizing Group Invitation Settings

By default, you will receive group invitations from your connections. If you don't want to receive these invitations, you can block them.

To do so, click the Settings link above the global navigation bar. On the Account & Settings page, click the Group Invitation Filtering link in the Groups section to open the Group Invitations Settings page.

This page offers two choices for handling group invitations:

- **I am open to receiving group invitations.** This is the default option that LinkedIn recommends.

- **I am not interested in receiving any group invitations.** LinkedIn blocks all future group invitations, and you no longer receive them.

Rather than blocking all group invitations, you can specify to view them online rather than receiving them by email. Refer to the section titled, "Customizing Email Notification Settings," earlier in this chapter, for more information.

To rearrange the order in which your groups display on the top navigation bar, click the Groups Order and Display link.

See Chapter 13, "Participating in LinkedIn Groups," for more information about creating and using LinkedIn groups.

Customizing Your LinkedIn Personal Information

To customize your LinkedIn personal information, click the Settings link above the global navigation bar.

The Personal Information section on the Account & Settings page provides links to modify the following data:

- **Name & Location.** Update your name and location. Additionally, specify the display name you want others to see. If you have strong privacy concerns, you can choose to display only your first name and last initial (such as Patrice R.) to people who aren't your connections. Displaying your full name will yield better results.

- **Email Addresses.** Add or delete email addresses and specify your primary email address where LinkedIn sends all messages. It's a good idea to enter all your active email addresses on the Email Addresses page. This includes your work email, personal email, and school email if you're a recent graduate or still use a university email account. When people invite you to connect, LinkedIn matches the email address they enter for you to your LinkedIn account. Entering all your email accounts helps ensure a match.

Remember that many LinkedIn features aren't available until you confirm your email address. If you haven't done so yet, or didn't receive your original confirmation email, you can request another confirmation message on this page.

- **Change Password.** Specify a new password to use. Changing passwords on occasion is a good security measure. Also, remember to create a strong password that includes a combination of uppercase and lowercase letters, numbers, and symbols.

- **Close Your Account.** Close your account and specify your reason for doing so. Keep in mind that if you choose this option, you'll lose all your LinkedIn connections and will no longer have access to the site.

Customizing Your Privacy Settings

LinkedIn enables you to specify privacy settings for the data you display on the LinkedIn site and for the way LinkedIn uses your personal information.

To learn more about LinkedIn's privacy policy, click the Privacy Policy link on LinkedIn's bottom navigation menu.

To customize your privacy settings, click the Settings link above the global navigation bar. Next, click one of the following links in the Privacy Settings section of the Account & Settings page:

- **Research Surveys.** Specify whether you want to receive invitations to participate in LinkedIn online market research surveys.

- **Connections Browse.** By default, LinkedIn allows your direct connections to browse a list of your other connections. This can provide a useful way to develop your network, as it's quite likely that you may know some of your connections' connections. If you want to hide your connections list, however, you can choose to do so on the Connections Browse page. Your connections will still be able to view shared connections, however.

- **Profile Views.** The LinkedIn home page displays a box titled Who's Viewed My Profile that provides information about the people who visit your profile. You can customize what, if anything, LinkedIn publishes about you when you visit a LinkedIn member's profile. Options include displaying your name and headline, anonymous profile characteristics (such as industry and title), or nothing at all. If you're using LinkedIn as a business development tool, you might want others to know that you visited their profile. Otherwise, you might prefer complete or partial anonymity.

- **Viewing Profile Photos.** You can choose whose photos you want to view. Options include all photos, no photos, or only photos of people in your network or people who are your connections.

To specify who can view *your* photo, go to the Account & Settings page and click the My Profile Photo link in the Profile Settings section.

- **Profile and Status Updates.** When you update your status, modify your profile, or make recommendations, LinkedIn notifies your connections of these changes and publishes them in company and industry updates. For most people, this provides good exposure on the LinkedIn network. If you want to block these notifications, however, you can do so. LinkedIn handles profile update notifications and status update notifications separately so you can choose to participate in one, both, or neither.

- **Service Provider Directory.** LinkedIn publishes a service provider directory for members who offer professional services. If another member recommends you, you can choose whether you want to be listed in the service provider directory. For most people, this is a great form of free publicity. If you're a corporate employee, however, you might not want to be included if you perform professional services only on occasion. See Chapter 15, "Using LinkedIn Service Providers," for more information about becoming a service provider.

- **NYTimes.com Customization.** LinkedIn shares non-personally identifiable profile information with the NYTimes.com to customize your experience on that site, including enhanced advertising. For example, if you select Banking as your industry, you'll view a customized list of headlines related to banking when you visit NYTimes.com. To opt out of this program, click the No button on the NYTimes.com Customization page.

- **Partner Advertising.** LinkedIn analyzes anonymous data from your profile, such as your industry, to customize the advertisements it displays and the content you view on partner sites (such as NYTimes.com). For example, if you specify Banking as your industry, you'll view ads that are relevant to professionals in that industry. If you don't want LinkedIn to use your personal data in this way, you can opt out of this service.

- **Authorized Applications.** The Authorized Applications page enables you to remove LinkedIn applications you installed. You can also remove access to external websites that you granted access to your LinkedIn data, such as Simply Hired or Business Exchange. See Chapter 12, "Enhancing Your Profile with LinkedIn Applications," for more information about how to use LinkedIn applications.

Customizing Your LinkedIn Network Options

The final section of the Account & Settings page enables you to let LinkedIn know how you plan to use your LinkedIn network. Click the Using Your Network link to provide LinkedIn with this informational data.

The options include the following:

- Find a job
- Find consulting or contracting positions
- Hire employees or contractors
- Sell products or services to companies
- Investigate deals with companies
- Find information about industries, products, or companies
- Find professionals interested in my new venture or product

This chapter explains the importance of maintaining a current profile and shows you how to ensure that your profile is up-to-date.

5

Maintaining Your LinkedIn Profile

Creating a solid profile is the first step in developing your presence on LinkedIn. After that, you need to continually maintain and update it to make the most of what LinkedIn has to offer.

In this chapter, you learn how to update and promote your LinkedIn profile, create a profile in another language, and print and download your profile. You can also listen to tips on keeping your profile current and watch videos that show you how to post updates, update your profile, and promote your profile on the Web.

Keeping Your Profile Current

Keeping your profile current is critical to your success on LinkedIn. Creating your initial profile may be a one-time task, but you need to update it regularly to let others know you're an active participant on LinkedIn. In addition to updating your actual profile, LinkedIn enables you to post frequent updates to inform your network about your activities and accomplishments.

 TELL ME MORE Media 5.1—Keeping Your LinkedIn Profile Current

Access this video file through your registered Web edition at
my.safaribooksonline.com/9780789745095/media.

Posting Updates

LinkedIn enables you to share important news with other LinkedIn members in text updates of up to 700 characters. You also can insert URLs in your updates with a title, description, and optional photo. For example, you could link to your website, a blog post, or an article on an external news site.

If you want to share your LinkedIn updates on Twitter, you should limit them to 140 characters; otherwise, only the first 140 characters of your update will display. See Chapter 2, "Creating Your LinkedIn Profile," for more information about integrating LinkedIn with Twitter.

Figure 5.1 shows an example of a brief text-only update suitable for cross-posting on Twitter.

Sara Wretstrom Just received my certificate in Social Media Marketing from the University of California, Irvine.

6 seconds ago · Comment · See all activity »

Figure 5.1   *Quickly let your connections know what's new in your professional life.*

Figure 5.2 shows an example of an update that includes a link to a blog posting.

Figure 5.2   *Showcase relevant blog posts with a LinkedIn update.*

When you post an update, it displays in several places:

- At the top of your profile just below your name and headline
- In the Activity section of your profile, located in the right sidebar
- In the Network Activity section of your home page
- In the Network Activity section of your connections' home page—if you choose to share with them

Your update remains indefinitely until you either delete it or replace it with a new update.

Although updates are a fun way to let your connections know what's new in your life, they are also a strategic networking tool. Keep your goals in mind and post updates that help achieve them. A well-crafted update can be an effective marketing and publicity tool, but be careful to avoid overt sales pitches in your updates. An update is a conversation with your network, not an advertisement.

Posting an Update

There are two places where you can post an update on LinkedIn—on your home page and on the Edit My Profile page.

SHOW ME   Media 5.2—Posting an Update on LinkedIn
Access this video file through your registered Web edition at
my.safaribooksonline.com/9780789745095/media.

If you post updates on multiple social networking sites, consider using a free service such as Ping.fm (http://ping.fm). Ping.fm enables you to simultaneously post updates to sites such as LinkedIn, Facebook, and Twitter.

LET ME TRY IT

Posting an Update on LinkedIn

To post an update on LinkedIn, follow these steps:

1. On the global navigation bar, select Edit Profile from the Profile drop-down menu.

2. On the Edit My Profile page, click the Post an Update link.

3. Enter your update in the box that appears, as shown in Figure 5.3. Remember that you can enter up to 700 characters unless you want to share your update on Twitter. In that case, you should limit your update to 140 characters (Twitter cuts off anything in excess of this length).

Optionally, scroll down to the Network Activity section on your home page to enter your update in an identical box that displays there.

Figure 5.3 *Use an update to let other LinkedIn members know what you're doing.*

4. If you want to refer to an external URL, click the Attach a Link link. If not, skip to step 10.

5. Enter the URL you want to include in the Add URL box, such as http:/ /www.patricerutledge.com/books/usinglinkedin.

6. Click the Attach button. LinkedIn searches for this URL and displays a title, description, and photo from this content it finds on this page (see Figure 5.4).

Figure 5.4 *Attach links to relevant external sites, such as a website, blog, or news site.*

7. Optionally, click the Edit link to make changes to this default content.

8. Enter any changes to the title or description in the text boxes. Remember that the description text displays in addition to what you enter in the update box.

9. The Include Photo checkbox is selected by default, but you can remove this checkmark if you don't want to include a photo. To change from the default photo, click the arrows below the photo to view alternative selections. LinkedIn searches for any photos on the page you're sharing and offers them as options here.

10. Click the down arrow to the right of the Visible To drop-down list to specify who can see this update. You can share with everyone on LinkedIn or only with your connections.

11. If you set up LinkedIn to integrate with Twitter, you can select the checkbox to the left of the Twitter button to share your update on Twitter. If you haven't set up LinkedIn Twitter integration yet, you're prompted to do so before continuing. See Chapter 2 for more information about setting up this integration.

12.   Click the Share button to post your update, as shown in Figure 5.5.

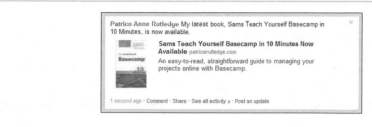

Figure 5.5   *An update as it displays on your profile.*

LinkedIn displays this update on your profile and home page. Your connections can also view this update on your profile and the Network Activity section of their home page. If you chose to share with everyone, any LinkedIn member who visits your home page can view your updates, but they won't appear on their home pages unless you connect with them.

Managing Your Updates

After posting an update, you can

- Delete the update by clicking the Delete Your Update button (a large X) in the upper-right corner of your update box.

- Share your update with groups to which you belong or individual connections by clicking the Share link below your update. Figure 5.6 shows the Share dialog box that opens.

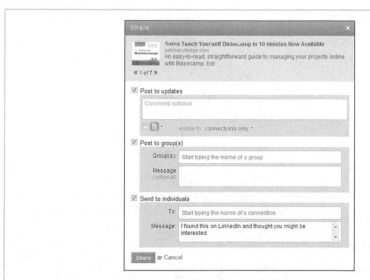

Figure 5.6   *Share your update with group members and individual connections.*

- View a list of your latest updates by clicking the See All Activity link below your update.

Commenting On an Update

When your update appears in your connections' Network Activity section on their home pages, they can enter their own comments by clicking the Comment link below your update. They can also send you a private message by clicking the Reply Privately link.

If your connections have entered comments about your update, you'll see a link beneath your posted update on your home page and on your profile. The link tells you how many comments you have (for example, 2 Comments). Click this link to view your comments and add your own feedback to the discussion.

Adding your own comments to your connections' updates is a good way to stay in touch and maintain visibility.

Updating Your Profile

Even if you create a thorough profile when you first sign up for LinkedIn, you'll eventually want to update it with recent information.

You should update your LinkedIn profile whenever you do the following:

- Change employers
- Become unemployed
- Get promoted
- Receive a degree or certification
- Join a new professional association
- Receive an award
- Learn new skills
- Change your LinkedIn goals
- Start a new business
- Create a new website or blog
- Complete a major project or career milestone

SHOW ME   Media 5.3—Updating Your LinkedIn Profile
Access this video file through your registered Web edition at
my.safaribooksonline.com/9780789745095/media.

To update your profile, select Edit Profile from the Profile drop-down menu on the global navigation bar. The Edit My Profile page opens, shown in Figure 5.7.

Figure 5.7   *Be sure to update your profile regularly with new information.*

The Edit My Profile page is the same place you first created your profile, so you should already be familiar with its content. After you first enter profile data, links such as Add Past Position or Add Education disappear. Instead, click the Edit link next to any field you want to update. The appropriate LinkedIn page opens, where you can make any required changes.

You can also click the Current, Past, Education, Recommended, Connections, and Websites links to enter data or make changes in those sections.

See Chapter 2 for more information about the content you can enter on the Edit My Profile page.

Although it's not necessary to update your profile every week, you shouldn't let it get outdated either. If it's obvious that you haven't touched your profile in months, or years, LinkedIn members might not bother contacting you for what could have been a lucrative opportunity for you.

Promoting Your Profile on the Web

With your permission, LinkedIn makes a public version of your profile available for view and search on the Web. Figure 5.8 shows a sample LinkedIn profile link in Google search results.

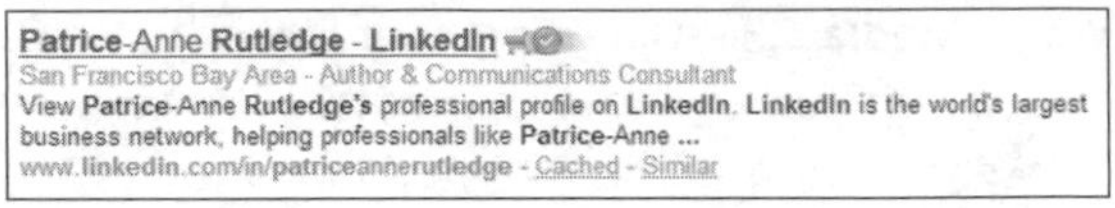

Patrice-Anne Rutledge - LinkedIn
San Francisco Bay Area - Author & Communications Consultant
View **Patrice-Anne Rutledge's** professional profile on **LinkedIn. LinkedIn** is the world's largest
business network, helping professionals like **Patrice-Anne** ...
www.linkedin.com/in/patriceannerutledge - Cached - Similar

Figure 5.8 *Your LinkedIn public profile appears in Google search results.*

Although promoting your profile online is most common, many LinkedIn members also print their LinkedIn profile URL on business cards, brochures, and other marketing materials.

 SHOW ME Media 5.4—Promoting Your Profile on the Web
Access this video file through your registered Web edition at
my.safaribooksonline.com/9780789745095/media.

To customize the appearance of your public profile, click the Settings link above the global navigation bar. On the Account & Settings page, click the Public Profile link.

Chapter 2 provided details on how to manage your public profile. As a reminder, here are tips to maximize your profile's online visibility:

- Customize your public profile URL to make it user-friendly, such as http:/
  /www.linkedin.com/in/patriceannerutledge.

- Select the Full View option on the Public Profile page and place a check mark next to all fields you want to appear on your public profile.

- Preview your public profile to ensure that you like how it appears to others on the Web.

In addition to maintaining a public profile, you can also post a LinkedIn button on your website, blog, or online resume. Figure 5.9 shows a sample button.

Figure 5.9 *Put a LinkedIn button on your website so your visitors can easily view your profile.*

Click the Customized Buttons link on the Public Profile page to open the Promote Your Profile! page, where you can select the button style you prefer. LinkedIn offers a special button for TypePad users, but you can place your button on any blog or website. For example, a blog sidebar is a great place for a LinkedIn button. Copy the HTML code LinkedIn provides and paste into your own site.

A third way to promote your LinkedIn profile on the Web is to include a link to your public profile URL on the following:

- Your email signature

- Your online business card

- Other social networking sites

If you use Facebook (www.facebook.com), consider installing the My LinkedIn Profile application on your Facebook profile.

Creating Profiles in Other Languages

English is the primary language on LinkedIn, but LinkedIn is a decidedly international network, with more than half its members residing outside the United States. In Europe, for example, LinkedIn is the number-one professional networking site in 43 countries. To meet the needs of its many international members, LinkedIn offers several foreign language features.

The LinkedIn interface is available in six languages: English, French, Spanish, German, Italian, and Portuguese. To view LinkedIn in another language, click the Language link on the bottom navigation menu and select your preferred language. Figure 5.10 shows the LinkedIn interface in French.

Figure 5.10 *The LinkedIn interface is available in French as well as five other languages.*

Keep in mind that even if you view the LinkedIn interface in another language, this doesn't translate the user-generated content of an individual member's profile. The profile content remains in the original language the member used to create it.

To display your profile content in another language, you need to create a profile in that language. For example, someone involved in international business or residing in a country with more than one official language might want to create profiles in multiple languages.

 LET ME TRY IT

Creating a Profile in Another Language

To create a profile in another language, follow these steps:

1. On the global navigation bar, select Edit Profile from the Profile drop-down menu.

2. Click the Create Your Profile in Another Language link, which appears at the top of the right column of the Edit My Profile page. The Create Your Profile in Another Language page opens, shown in Figure 5.11.

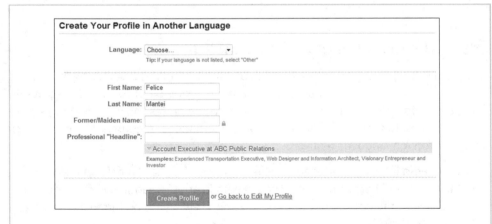

Figure 5.11   *Create your profile in more than 40 supported languages.*

3. Select the language for your profile from the Language drop-down list. LinkedIn currently supports more than 40 languages. To create a profile in a language that LinkedIn doesn't support, select Other.

4. Enter your first name, last name, and a former/maiden name, if applicable.

5. Enter your professional headline.

6. Click the Create Profile button to return to the Edit My Profile page.

7. Enter your profile content in your target language, just as you did for your English-language profile.

LinkedIn members can choose to view your profile in another language by select-ing their preferred language from the Profile drop-down list in the upper-right cor-ner of your profile, shown in Figure 5.12.

Figure 5.12   *Members can choose to view your profile content in any of the language versions you create.*

Only those languages for which you create a profile are available in the drop-down list. If you have a profile only in English, the Profile field won't be visible.

Printing and Downloading Your Profile

You can print and download your profile, or the profile of another LinkedIn mem-ber, by clicking one of the icons in the upper-right corner of a profile, shown in Figure 5.13.

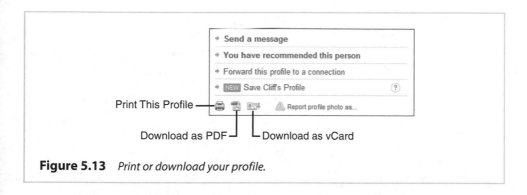

Figure 5.13   *Print or download your profile.*

Your options include the following:

- **Print This Profile.** Opens the Print dialog box where you can specify print options and print a profile.

- **Download as PDF.** Creates a PDF document from your profile that you can view with Adobe Reader (get.adobe.com/reader).

- **Download vCard.** Downloads your profile in the vCard format, which is a file format used for electronic business cards. This option appears only for your own profile or for your connections.

If you use Internet Explorer, the Bookmark Using the IE Toolbar icon also appears.

This chapter introduces you to the LinkedIn network and the many ways to communicate with other LinkedIn members.

6

Communicating with Your LinkedIn Network

Before you start communicating with others on LinkedIn, you need to understand how LinkedIn classifies its members in terms of their connection to you. This distinction is important because it determines what, if any, restrictions LinkedIn places on your ability to contact people.

In this chapter, you learn about LinkedIn's three levels of connection, sending messages and InMail, working with the introduction process, and managing your Inbox. You can also listen to tips on how to maximize the potential of your LinkedIn network and watch videos that show you how to send a message, request an introduction, and manage introduction requests.

Understanding Your LinkedIn Network

Your LinkedIn network consists of three levels of connections:

- **1st-degree connections.** LinkedIn members you connect with directly. Either you sent them an invitation to connect and they accepted, or you accepted their invitation. Your connection list on your profile displays your 1st-degree connections. When LinkedIn refers to "your connections," this means your 1st-degree connections.

- **2nd-degree connections.** LinkedIn members who connect directly with your 1st-degree connections but aren't your 1st-degree connections.

- **3rd-degree connections.** LinkedIn members who connect directly with your 2nd-degree connections but aren't your 1st- or 2nd-degree connections.

 TELL ME MORE   Media 6.1—The LinkedIn Network

Access this audio recording through your registered Web Edition at
my.safaribooksonline.com/9780789745095/media.

For example, if you connect directly with your colleague Amanda, she is your 1st-degree connection. If Amanda connects directly to Justin, her former classmate, Justin is your 2nd-degree connection. If Justin connects directly with Blake, one of his co-workers, Blake is your 3rd-degree connection.

LinkedIn also considers fellow members of groups as part of your network. See Chapter 13, "Participating in LinkedIn Groups," for more information about LinkedIn groups.

To view how many people are in each level of your network, select Network Statistics from the Contacts drop-down menu on the global navigation bar.

Your LinkedIn network (termed "My Network") differs from the entire LinkedIn network, which consists of all LinkedIn members. At the time of this printing, the entire LinkedIn network includes more than 65 million members.

Understanding LinkedIn Messages, InMail, and Introductions

LinkedIn offers several ways to communicate with other members. The type of communication you can send depends on how you're connected to these members. Your choices include the following:

- **Messages.** Messages are the primary form of communication on LinkedIn. You can send messages to your direct connections as well as to the people who belong to the same LinkedIn groups as you do. If you can send a message to someone, the Send Message link appears next to their name on their profile and in search results. See "Sending and Managing Messages" later in this chapter for more information. Although you'll often see the term "message" used generically to refer to all items in your Inbox, it is a specific type of communication in itself.

- **Invitations.** An invitation is a request to connect with another LinkedIn member. See Chapter 3, "Developing Your LinkedIn Network," for more information about sending invitations.

- **InMail.** An InMail is a private message to or from a LinkedIn member who is not your connection. You can receive InMail free if you indicate that you are open to receiving InMail messages on the Account & Settings page. In general, sending InMail is a paid LinkedIn feature unless the recipient is a premium member who belongs to the OpenLink Network. See "Sending InMail" later in this chapter for more information.

- **Introductions.** An introduction provides a way to reach out to the people who are connected to your connections. By requesting an introduction through someone you already know, that person can introduce you to the person you're trying to reach. You can contact your 1st-degree connections to request introductions to members who are 2nd- and 3rd-degree connections. Members with free accounts can have up to five introductions open at a time. See "Requesting Introductions" later in this chapter for more information.

Understanding Your Contact Options

Before you start communicating with another LinkedIn member, you need to understand your available options for contacting that particular person. When you view member profiles or their summary information from another part of the site, the icons next to a member's name tell you how you're connected (see Figure 6.1).

Figure 6.1   *The icons next to a member's name tell you how you're connected.*

These icons identify 1st-, 2nd-, and 3rd-degree connections, fellow group members, and LinkedIn premium account holders.

Members who display no icons next to their names are out of your network, don't share any groups, and aren't premium account holders.

The links that display to the right of a member's name let you know what contact options are available. These include the following:

- **Send a Message.** Send a message to a direct connection or group member.

- **Send InMail.** Send an InMail to someone who isn't in your network. This option doesn't appear for members to whom you can send a message because it wouldn't make sense to pay to contact someone you can communicate with freely. If you click the Send InMail link and don't have a premium account, LinkedIn prompts you to sign up for one before you can proceed.

- **Send InMail (Free).** Send an OpenLink message to a member of the OpenLink Network. LinkedIn members who hold premium accounts can offer you the option of sending them free InMail. See Chapter 1 for more information about the OpenLink Network.

- **Recommend This Person.** Post a recommendation for this LinkedIn member.

- **You Have Recommended This Person.** View the recommendation you posted.

- **Get Introduced Through a Connection.** Request an introduction to this member through a 1st-degree connection.

- **Add [First Name] to Your Network.** Send an invitation to connect. See Chapter 3, "Developing Your LinkedIn Network," for more information about sending connection requests.

- **Forward This Profile to a Connection.** Forward a member's profile to a member you know, as a way of informal introduction.

- **Search for References/Find References.** Search for LinkedIn members who worked at the same company at the same time as this member.

- **Save [First Name]'s Profile.** Save this person's profile to your Profile Organizer (a premium feature). See Chapter 7, "Searching for People on LinkedIn," for more information.

These are the link names that appear on an actual profile. The link names in search results are sometimes abbreviated.

Remember that you'll never see all of these options for any one member. For example, it wouldn't make sense to send InMail, request an introduction, or add to your network a member who is already your connection, so these options don't appear for your connections.

Managing Your Inbox

Your Inbox is the focal point for all your direct communication on LinkedIn. A summary of your five most recent Inbox items appears at the top of your home page. You can also click the Inbox link on the global navigation bar to open the Inbox ze, shown in Figure 6.2.

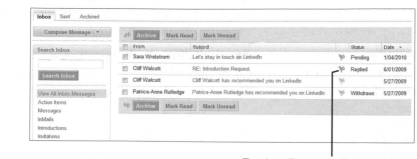

Toggle to flag and unflag action items.

Figure 6.2   *Your Inbox is the focal point for your personal communications on LinkedIn.*

The default view of your Inbox is the Inbox tab, which displays all the items you've received. If you have a lot of Inbox items and want to filter what you see, click one of the links below the search box to narrow your choices. For example, you can choose to display only action items, messages, InMails, introductions, invitations, profiles, jobs, recommendations, or group messages.

In addition to filtering Inbox items, you can also search for a specific message. Enter a keyword in the text box on the left side of the page and click the Search Inbox button. LinkedIn displays all messages containing that search term. For example, you could search for a person's name or a word or phrase in the subject line or message text.

From the Inbox, you can do the following:

- **Sort your messages.** Click one of the message headings (From, Subject, Status, or Date) to sort based on that heading.

- **Archive a message.** Select the checkbox to the left of the message you want to move to the Archive folder and click the Archive button. It's a good idea to archive old or resolved messages to keep your Inbox focused on your current action items.

LinkedIn doesn't let you delete messages from your Inbox. If you want to remove messages, simply archive the messages you no longer need to view.

- **Mark a message as read or unread.** By default, new messages appear in bold text to signify they have not yet been read. After you read a message, the message no longer is boldfaced in your Inbox. To change this, select the checkbox to the left of a message and click either the Mark Read button or Mark Unread button.

- **Flag a message as an action item for follow-up.** By default, new messages include a flag icon to the right of the subject line, flagging it as an action item. Click the flag icon, which serves as a toggle, to flag or unflag a message for action.

The Inbox also includes two other tabs. The Sent tab displays all your sent messages, and the Archived tab displays all the messages you archived.

You can also access each tab of your Inbox from the Inbox drop-down menu on the global navigation bar.

Each message also lists a status. When a new message arrives, its status displays as Pending. Based on the action you take on each message, your status changes. Status options include

- **Accepted.** You accepted the message, such as an invitation to connect.

- **Bounced.** The message bounced when sent to an email provider.

- **Don't Know/Doesn't Know.** The message, such as an invitation to connect, was rejected when the recipient clicked the I Don't Know This User button. LinkedIn lists the status as "Don't Know" if you clicked the button. The status is "Doesn't Know" if you sent the request that was rejected.

- **In Progress/Pending.** Identifies an InMail or request that is still an action item for one of the people involved.

- **Replaced.** Another message has replaced this message, and you can no longer respond to it. For example, someone sent you a recommendation request and then resent it when you didn't respond.

- **Replied.** You replied to the message.

- **Sent.** You sent this message. If the message was a request, the recipient hasn't accepted it yet.

- **Withdrawn.** The sender has withdrawn this message, request, or invitation.

You can also send messages directly from the Inbox. Click the Compose Message button to open the Compose Your Message page and send a message to a connection. For other options, click the down arrow to the right of the Compose Message button. From the drop-down list, you can choose to do the following:

- Send a message to a connection (the same result as clicking the Compose Message button)
- Send InMail or an introduction
- Send an invitation
- Send a recommendation
- Request a recommendation
- Send a job notification

Refer to other sections in this chapter and other chapters in this book for more information about each specific type of communication.

Sending and Managing Messages

Messages are the most common form of communication on LinkedIn. They're free and enable you to stay in touch with your connections.

Sending Messages

 SHOW ME   Media 6.2—Sending a Message in LinkedIn
Access this video file through your registered Web Edition at
my.safaribooksonline.com/9780789745095/media.

 LET ME TRY IT

Sending a Message

To send a message to a 1st-degree connection or group member, follow these steps:

1. On the global navigation bar, select Compose Message from the Inbox drop-down menu to open the Compose Your Message page, shown in Figure 6.3.

2. In the To field, start typing the name of your connection and wait for LinkedIn to find a match.

Start typing a name to find a match.

Compose your message   You can add 50 more connections

To: Pa|

Patrice-Anne Rutledge
Author & Communications Consultant

From: cliff_walcott@yahoo.com

Subject:

Figure 6.3 *Sending a direct message to one of your LinkedIn connections.*

Alternatively, click the Address Book icon to open your connection list. With the address book, you can search for the person you want to reach or select multiple recipients for your message. LinkedIn enables you to send a message to up to 50 connections at one time.

3. Enter a subject for your message.

4. Enter your message in the text box.

5. If you're sending a message to multiple recipients and don't want to disclose this information, remove the checkmark before the Allow Recipients to See Each Other's Names and Email Addresses checkbox (selected by default).

6. To email yourself a copy of your message, select the Send Me a Copy checkbox. Your message already appears in your Sent folder by default.

7. Click the Send button. LinkedIn sends your message to the recipient and notifies you that your message was sent.

Although clicking the Compose Message link is the primary way to send messages on LinkedIn, you can also send messages by clicking the Send a Message link in a profile, on your home page, or in search results.

The profiles of your direct connections also display their external email address in the Contact Information box on the right side of their profile. Some members include their email addresses directly on their profiles for the entire LinkedIn network to see.

Reading and Replying to Messages

You can open your messages from the Inbox preview on your home page or from the Inbox itself (access it by clicking the Inbox link on the global navigation bar).

Click the Subject line link of any message to open it. Figure 6.4 illustrates a sample message.

Figure 6.4   *View a message and reply to it.*

The buttons that appear at the bottom of a message vary depending upon the message type and what actions you can take. For example, a basic message includes the Reply button, a recommendation request includes the Write Recommendation button, and an invitation to connect includes the Accept button and I Don't Know This User button.

Sending InMail

As you learned earlier in this chapter, InMail enables you to contact LinkedIn members who aren't in your network. In an effort to manage spam, LinkedIn requires members to pay to send InMail. InMail is most useful for members who want to contact a wide variety of people, such as recruiters or individuals using LinkedIn for business development.

LinkedIn premium accounts, including Job Seeker premium accounts, enable you to send a fixed number of InMail messages per month. To learn more about LinkedIn premium accounts and InMail, click the Upgrade Your Account link on the bottom navigation menu. To learn more about Job Seeker premium accounts, select Job Seeker Premium from the Jobs drop-down menu on the global navigation bar.

You can also purchase individual InMails at $10 each. To do so, click the Settings link on the global navigation bar and then click the Purchase link in the Account section. This is cost-efficient only if you want to contact just a few people by InMail.

If you see the word "Free" immediately following a Send InMail link, you can send InMail to this LinkedIn member at no charge. To enable members to send you free InMail, you must participate in the OpenLink Network, a premium feature.

See Chapter 1 to learn more about the OpenLink Network and premium account options. See Chapter 9 to learn more about Job Seeker premium accounts.

To determine the InMail options available for a particular member, view the contact options on that person's profile (see Figure 6.5).

You can send free InMail to this member.

> ⊕ **Send InMail** Free
> ⊕ **Get introduced through a connection**
> ⊕ **Add John to your network**
> ⊕ Forward this profile to a connection
> ⊕ NEW Save John's Profile   ⑦

Figure 6.5   *Determine the InMail options for a particular LinkedIn member.*

You won't see any Send InMail link for members who indicate on the Account & Settings page that they aren't open to receiving InMail. InMail isn't an option for your connections, either. You can contact them directly at no cost to either party.

 **LET ME TRY IT**

Sending InMail to a LinkedIn Member

To send InMail to a LinkedIn member, follow these steps:

1. Click the Send InMail link on the profile of the person you want to reach. If you're sending paid InMail, the Compose Your Message page opens. If you're sending free InMail, the Compose Your OpenLink Message page opens (see Figure 6.6). These pages contain identical information.

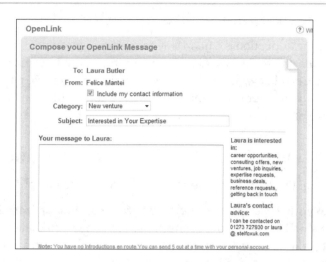

Figure 6.6 *Sending free InMail to members of the OpenLink Network.*

2. If you don't want to share your contact information with the person you want to reach, remove the checkmark from the Include My Contact Information checkbox (selected by default). In general, it's a good idea to share contact information.

3. In the Category drop-down list, select the reason for your InMail. Options include: career opportunity, consulting offer, new venture, job inquiry, expertise request, business deal, reference request, or get back in touch.

4. In the Subject field, enter the subject of your InMail.

5. In the text box, enter your message. To increase your chances of a positive reply, be as specific as possible.

6. Click the Send button to send your InMail. If the recipient doesn't respond to the InMail within seven days, the message expires.

For more information about InMail, refer to "Understanding InMail, Introductions, and LinkedIn Messages" in this chapter, and see Chapter 1.

Although InMail is an effective LinkedIn communication tool, it comes at a price. If you want to contact someone you don't know and don't want to pay to send InMail, you have several other options. You could join a group that this person belongs to and then send a message or invitation to connect as a fellow group member. You could also request an introduction through a mutual connection. Alternatively, you could choose to contact the individual outside LinkedIn by accessing the website links and external email information individuals provide on their profiles.

Requesting and Managing Introductions

Requesting an introduction is a good way to reach people in your network whom you don't connect with directly. Although you can send an invitation to connect to someone you don't know, for important communications you might want to consider requesting an introduction through a shared connection. An introduction can carry more weight than a cold contact.

Maximizing the Power of LinkedIn Introductions

Here are several tips for making the most of LinkedIn introductions:

- **Talk to your 1st-degree connection before sending an introduction request on LinkedIn.** Your connection might have information that's pertinent to your request. For example, if you're trying to reach someone about job opportunities, your connection might know if your target is hiring or if there's a more suitable person to contact.

- **Focus on introductions to 2nd-degree connections for best results.** Although you can request an introduction to a 3rd-degree connection, this requires two intermediaries. In many cases, the second intermediary (your 2nd-degree connection passing on your request to your 3rd-degree connection) might not even know you.

- **Make your introduction request concise and specific.** A vague request to "get to know" someone isn't nearly as effective as stating your specific purpose, such as seeking employment, recruiting for a job, offering consulting services, and so forth.

- **Keep in mind that you can have only five open introductions at one time with a free LinkedIn personal account.** Find out how many introductions you still have available by clicking the Settings link on the global navigation bar and viewing your account summary. To increase your number of open introductions, you need to upgrade to a premium account. LinkedIn recommends using introductions judiciously rather than as a tool to contact hundreds of members.

Requesting Introductions

Before you send your first introduction request, it's important to understand how the process works. For example, let's say that you're connected to your former manager, Marianne (1st-degree connection), and Marianne is connected to Dalton (2nd-degree connection), a manager at another local company. You're very interested in working in Dalton's department, but you don't know him and haven't seen any posted job openings. Rather than sending Dalton an email and resume as a "cold contact," you could send an introduction request through Marianne.

Often you'll already know how you're connected to the person you want to reach, but you can also determine this by viewing the How You're Connected To [First Name] on your target contact's profile. If you don't already know of a common connection, this box could list a name you recognize.

SHOW ME   Media 6.3—Requesting Introductions in LinkedIn
Access this video file through your registered Web Edition at
my.safaribooksonline.com/9780789745095/media.

LET ME TRY IT

Requesting an Introduction

To request an introduction, follow these steps:

1. Click the Get Introduced Through a Connection link on the profile of the person you want to reach. The Introductions page opens, shown in Figure 6.7.

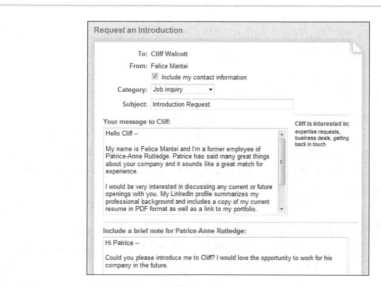

Figure 6.7   *Requesting an introduction to someone your connection knows.*

You can also request an introduction by clicking the Get Introduced link in search results or group member lists.

2. If you don't want to share your contact information with the person you want to reach, remove the checkmark from the Include My Contact Information checkbox (selected by default). LinkedIn shares your email address and an optional phone number.

3. From the Category drop-down list, select the reason for your introduction request. Options include career opportunity, consulting offer, new venture, job inquiry, expertise request, business deal, reference request, or get back in touch.

4. In the Subject field, enter the subject of your request.

5. In the first text box, enter your message to the person you want to be introduced to.

6. In the second text box, enter a brief note to the person you want to make the referral (your 1st-degree connection).

7. Click the Send button to send your introduction request.

Your 1st-degree connection receives your request and can choose to forward it to your target connection with comments or decline your request. If your request wasn't clear, your connection might ask you for more information.

See the following section, "Managing Introduction Requests," for more information about the next step in the process.

Managing Introduction Requests

If you send an introduction request, it's a good idea to understand the next steps in the process. In addition, you'll need to know how to manage the introduction requests other LinkedIn members send to you. For example, someone might ask you to facilitate an introduction to one of your connections or might ask your connection to facilitate an introduction to you.

 SHOW ME   Media 6.4—Managing LinkedIn Introduction Requests
Access this video file through your registered Web Edition at
my.safaribooksonline.com/9780789745095/media.

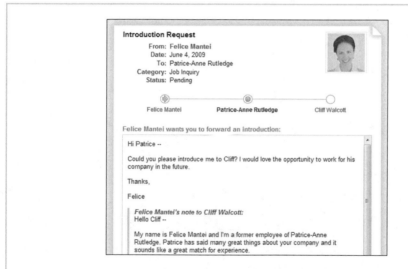

LET ME TRY IT

Responding to an Introduction Request

To review and respond to introduction requests, follow these steps:

1. On the global navigation bar, click the Inbox link to open your Inbox.

2. If you have many messages in your Inbox, click the Introductions link below the search box. Your Inbox displays only your introduction requests. Alternatively, you can also view new introduction requests in your Inbox preview on your home page or receive them by email (specify this on the Account & Settings page).

3. To open the request, click the Subject Line link. Figure 6.8 illustrates a sample introduction request.

Figure 6.8   *Forward an introduction request to one of your connections.*

4. Click the Forward Introduction button to forward the request to your connection.

If you don't want to make the introduction, click the Decline to Forward button. Alternatively, click the Archive button to move the request to your Archive folder where you can take action on the request later. Introduction requests remain active for six months.

5.   Enter any additional comments in the text box and click the Forward
     Message button.

The target recipient receives your forwarded introduction request and can accept,
decline, or archive it. Accepting the introduction enables the requestor and target
to communicate with each other, but they still need to send an invitation request
to become connections.

This chapter introduces you to LinkedIn's powerful
people search capabilities.

7

Searching for People on LinkedIn

LinkedIn is a large, complex network of information. You can greatly improve your chances of achieving your networking goals by learning how to find exactly what you want among millions of member profiles and many more millions of answers, job postings, and group discussions.

In this chapter, you explore the many ways to search for people on LinkedIn, including performing both quick and advanced searches as well as saving profiles for future reference. You can also listen to some easy search tips and watch videos that show you how to search for people, save a people search, and use the Profile Organizer.

Performing Quick Searches

The easiest way to search for information on LinkedIn is to use the search box on LinkedIn's global navigation bar, shown in Figure 7.1.

Figure 7.1   *Quickly search for information from anywhere on LinkedIn.*

 TELL ME MORE   Media 7.1—Performing Quick Searches on LinkedIn

Access this audio recording through your registered Web Edition at
my.safaribooksonline.com/9780789745095/media.

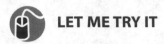 **LET ME TRY IT**

Performing a Quick Search

To perform a quick search, follow these steps:

1. Select the focus of your search from the drop-down list. Options include the following:

   - People (the default)
   - Jobs
   - Companies
   - Answers
   - Inbox
   - Groups

2. Enter your search term in the text box. This might be a person's name, company name, job title, job skill, or a keyword, for example.

3. Click the Search button (a small blue magnifying glass). LinkedIn displays search results. The format of the search results depends on the type of search you perform.

This chapter focuses on LinkedIn's most popular search type (the people search), as well as advanced search techniques. To learn more about searching for jobs, companies, answers, your Inbox, and groups, refer to the chapters in this book that cover those topics.

Searching for People

The fastest way to search for people is to perform a quick search from the search box on LinkedIn's top navigation menu. For example, let's say that you're searching for your former colleague, Felice Mantei. Enter her name in the search box and click the Search button. Your search results appear, as shown in Figure 7.2.

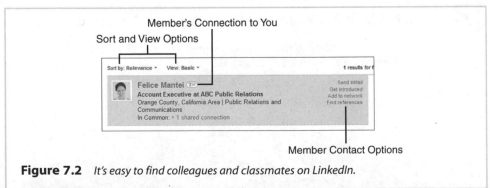

Figure 7.2 *It's easy to find colleagues and classmates on LinkedIn.*

SHOW ME   Media 7.2—Searching for People on LinkedIn
*Access this video file through your registered Web Edition at
my.safaribooksonline.com/9780789745095/media.*

As you type, LinkedIn displays a drop-down list of potential matches in your network of connections. If you see a match in this list, click the member's name to open that member's profile.

Each LinkedIn member who matches your search results appears in a preview box that includes a photo, name, headline, location, industry, and information about shared connections and groups. Depending on the preview you're viewing, not all items might appear. For example, a member might choose not to upload a photo.

Icons appear to the right of each member's name indicating their connection to you, such as a 1st-degree connection, 2nd-degree connection, 3rd-degree connection, or group member. For members who are out of your network, you may view the Out of Network designation next to their name, or their name may be hidden from view.

See Chapter 6, "Communicating with Your LinkedIn Network," for a reminder of how LinkedIn classifies its members.

Hover over the preview of a specific LinkedIn member to view the available contact links (the preview box turns blue). Possible links include Send Message, Get Introduced, Send InMail, Add to Network, or Save Profile. The options available depend on your connection to the particular member. For example, it wouldn't make sense for you to send InMail or get introduced to someone with whom you are already connected. See Chapter 6 for more information about the available options for contacting others on LinkedIn.

With a personal account, you can view 100 results at a time. To view more results, you need to upgrade to a premium account. To learn more about premium accounts, click the Upgrade Your Account link on the bottom navigation menu.

Narrowing People Search Results

When you search for the name of a specific individual, the search results should display a short list (unless the individual has a very common name). But what if you can't remember someone's last name or you're searching for LinkedIn members who meet specific criteria, such as CPAs in the Indianapolis area? In this case, your search might return thousands of results, exceeding the 100-result viewing limits associated with a personal account.

There are two ways to handle this. One is to narrow the results that display on your search results page. The other is to perform an advanced search that targets very specific criteria.

On the search results page, you can sort the search results using the following criteria:

- **Relevance.** Displays search results in the order LinkedIn determines most appropriate based on keywords you enter and your network.

- **Relationship.** Displays search results based on their position in your network, in the following order: 1st-degree connections, 2nd-degree connections, fellow group members, and 3rd-degree connections that are combined with out-of-network connections.

- **Relationship + Recommendations.** Displays search results by relationship. Those that have the most recommendations are listed first for each relationship category.

- **Connections.** Displays search results based on the number of common connections.

- **Keywords.** Displays search results that match your keywords without considering their placement in your network.

You also can customize the member information you preview in your search results. The options are as follows:

- **Basic.** Displays a photo, name, professional headline, location, industry, and details about shared connections.

- **Expanded.** Displays all the information from the basic view, as well as current and past employment details.

- **Create a New View.** Opens the Create a New View pop-up box (see Figure 7.3) in which you can specify the exact information you want to display in the preview. Options include the data you can see in Basic and Expanded views, as well as recommendations, groups, and number of connections. Click the

Save button to save your customized view for future use. Customized views are a premium feature for customers who upgrade to a paid account.

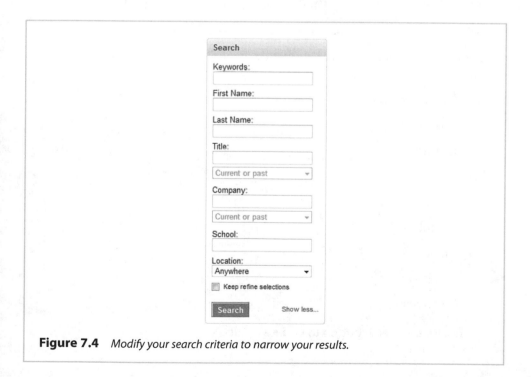

Figure 7.3 *Customize exactly what you see in search results.*

In the Search box, click the Show More link to display more options for narrowing your search, as shown in Figure 7.4.

Figure 7.4 *Modify your search criteria to narrow your results.*

In this box, you can narrow your search results by specifying any of the following criteria:

- **Keywords.** Enter a keyword that LinkedIn searches for in member profiles. The best keywords are terms that don't fit any of the other search criteria and are specific words that a member might include on a profile. For example, entering a name or location wouldn't be appropriate here, but terms such as Java, PMP, auditing, CPA, and so forth would work well.

- **First Name.** Enter the first name of the member you want to find.

- **Last Name.** Enter the last name of the member you want to find.

- **Title.** Enter a job title and specify in the drop-down list whether you want to search only for members who hold this title currently, in the past, or both currently and in the past.

- **Company.** Enter a company name and specify in the drop-down list whether you want to search only for members who work at this company currently, in the past, or both currently and in the past.

- **School.** Enter the name of a college or university.

- **Location.** Select a country, optional postal code, and distance range.

Click the Search button to update the search results.

For even more search options, consider the choices in the Filter By box (below the Search box):

- Current Company
- Relationship
- Industry
- Location
- Past Company
- School
- Groups
- Profile Language
- When Joined

Again, click the Search button to update results.

Performing Advanced People Searches

If you want to search for very specific criteria, you can perform an advanced people search. An advanced search offers you the same options as the extended version of the Search box on the search results page, but you can perform it all in one step. For example, you might enter a search term in the quick search box and then decide to narrow your results. But if you already know that you want to search for specific keywords, companies, or locations, for example, an advanced search is a more streamlined option.

To perform an advanced people search, select the People option (if it's not already selected by default) on the search box that appears on the global navigation bar and click the Advanced link. Figure 7.5 shows the Advanced People Search page.

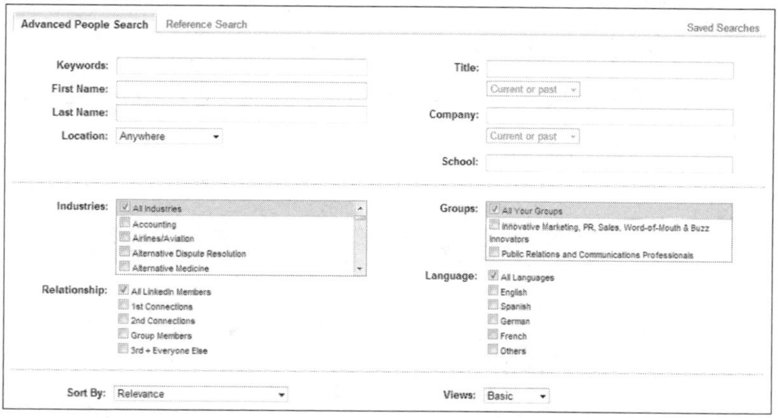

Figure 7.5 *LinkedIn's advanced search options provide maximum flexibility in finding members who meet specific criteria.*

Enter your search criteria on this page and click the Search button to display your search results. Refer to "Narrowing Your People Search Results," earlier in this chapter, for descriptions of each field on this page.

The Advanced People Search page also includes a Reference Search tab where you can search for potential references for a job candidate. See Chapter 11, "Recruiting Job Candidates," for more information about reference searches.

Saving People Searches

If you perform the same searches frequently, saving them can reduce redundant data entry.

 SHOW ME   Media 7.3—Saving a People Search on LinkedIn
Access this video file through your registered Web Edition at
my.safaribooksonline.com/9780789745095/media.

 LET ME TRY IT

Saving a People Search

To save a search for future use, follow these steps:

1. Click the Save link on the search results page.

2. In the Save pop-up box, enter a search name for this search (see Figure 7.6).

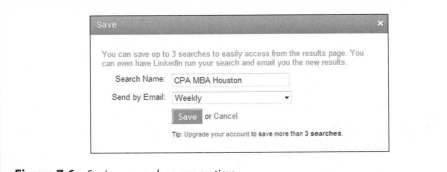

Figure 7.6   *Saving a search saves you time.*

3. In the Send by Email field, choose to receive email updates of your search results: Weekly, Monthly, or Never. You don't have to receive updates by email, but this can be a timesaver if you're very interested in following updates to your saved search. For example, recruiters might want to know about new LinkedIn members who match specific search criteria. Or, job seekers might want to know about new LinkedIn members who work at companies they're interested in working for.

As a free Personal account holder, you can save up to three searches and receive email updates either weekly or monthly. To save more searches, click the Upgrade Your Account link to sign up for a premium account. If you want to receive daily email updates on your saved searches, you must select the Pro account option.

   4. Click the Save button to save your search.

To edit or delete your saved searches, click the Saved Searches tab on the search results page.

Using Advanced Search Techniques

LinkedIn offers several techniques for narrowing your search results even further. You can use these techniques when performing a quick search or when using the Advanced Search page. For more targeted search results, try one of the following search types:

- **Quoted Searches.** To search for an exact phrase, use quotation marks before and after that phrase. For example, a search on "business analyst" returns only those profiles with this exact phrase.

- **NOT Searches.** To search for one term while excluding another, place the uppercase word NOT before the term you want to exclude. For example, searching for analyst NOT Oracle returns a list of members who include the word "analyst" in their profiles, but they do not include the word "Oracle" in their profiles.

- **OR Searches.** To search for two or more terms and display results for any of these terms, use the uppercase word OR between your search terms. For example, a search for Java OR PHP OR SQL finds profiles that include any (but not all) of these terms.

- **AND Searches.** To search for two or more terms and display results for all of these terms, use the uppercase word AND between your search terms. For example, a search for CPA AND MBA finds members with both qualifications.

When you search for two or more terms without using quotation marks, LinkedIn automatically performs an AND search by default. For example, entering **engineer MCSE** produces the same search result as entering **engineer AND MCSE.**

- **Parenthetical Searches.** To perform more complex searches involving AND and OR operators, use parentheses to separate your search terms. For example, let's say that you want to search for someone at either Yahoo! or Microsoft, but you want to limit your search results to Microsoft employees involved only with advertising. Your search phrase would be Yahoo OR (Microsoft AND advertising).

LinkedIn enables you to use specific search operators to define advanced criteria directly in the quick search box. For example, ccompany is the operator for current company and title is the operator for job title. Entering ccompany:Google title:director would quickly list all current Google employees with the title of director. To view a complete list of operators, select Learning Center from the More drop-down list on the global navigation bar. Then click the Search link to view a detailed list of operators.

Using the Profile Organizer

LinkedIn's Profile Organizer enables you to save profiles of interest, sort them into folders, and add notes about your contact with the members whose profiles you save.

You must have a premium LinkedIn account or sign up for a free Profile Organizer trial to use the Profile Organizer. The Business account plan and trial enable you to maintain five profile folders. With the Business Plus or Pro plans, you can maintain up to 25 folders.

 SHOW ME   Media 7.4—Using the LinkedIn Profile Organizer
Access this video file through your registered Web Edition at
my.safaribooksonline.com/9780789745095/media.

On the global navigation bar, select Profile Organizer from the Contacts drop-down menu to open the Profile Organizer page.

Figure 7.7 shows the Profile Organizer as it appears to LinkedIn members who haven't signed up yet.

Click the Upgrade Now button to upgrade to a paid account immediately or click the Start Free Trial link to receive a 30-day free trial of the Profile Organizer. No credit card is required for the free trial.

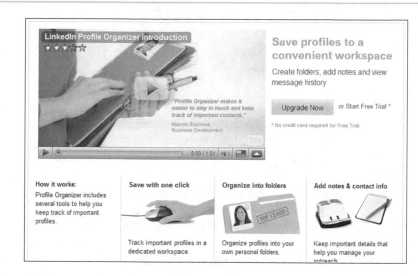

Figure 7.7   *Sign up for a free trial to try out the Profile Organizer.*

Free alternatives to the Profile Organizer include the Bookmark Profile features available with the LinkedIn Firefox browser toolbar and the LinkedIn Internet Explorer toolbar. Although bookmarking profiles in your browser doesn't offer the advanced features and flexibility of the Profile Organizer, it is a viable alternative for those on a tight budget.

Saving Profiles to the Profile Organizer

To save an open profile to the Profile Organizer, click the Save [First Name's] Profile link on the right side of the screen (see Figure 7.8). Alternatively, click the Save Profile link that appears to the right of a profile preview in search results.

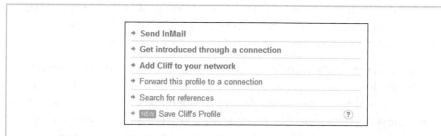

Figure 7.8   *Save a profile to the Profile Organizer with one click.*

LinkedIn saves the profile to the Profile Organizer and displays the Profile Organizer box on this member's profile, shown in Figure 7.9.

Figure 7.9   *Add this profile to a folder or enter your own notes.*

In the Profile Organizer box, you can do the following:

- Add this person's profile to a folder by clicking the Add [First Name] to a Folder link. You can add this profile to an existing folder or create a new folder.

- Enter contact information for this person by clicking the Contact Information link.

- Add a note of up to 1,000 characters in the text box.

Managing Profiles in the Profile Organizer

You can open the Profile Organizer by selecting Profile Organizer from the Contacts drop-down menu on the global navigation bar or clicking the Go to Profile Organizer link in the Profile Organizer box on a member profile. Figure 7.10 shows the Profile Organizer of a member using the trial plan.

In the Profile Organizer, you can do the following:

- **Add and view notes about each person whose profile you saved.** Notes can contain up to 1,000 characters. This is a good place to flag profiles for follow-up, indicate where you met a particular contact, and so forth.

- **Add profiles to folders.** LinkedIn provides the Folder 1 and Top Prospects folders by default, but you can change these folder names and add other folders. For example, you might want to create folders for potential recruitment prospects, potential clients, people you met at a conference, hiring managers at companies you want to work for, and so forth. Click the Add to Folder link below a person's name to add this profile to a folder. Click the Manage link on the right side of the screen to edit, rename, add, and delete folders.

Figure 7.10 *Save profiles you want to view again.*

- **Contact a LinkedIn member whose profile you saved.** To view potential options, mouse over the profile and view the contact options on the right side of the profile preview box. Depending on your connection to the person and what actions you've already taken, possible options include the following links: Send Message, Send InMail, Add Contact Info, Contact Information, Add a Note, and Archive.

Archiving removes a profile from your main Profile Organizer view. This is useful for profiles you want to retain, but don't need immediate attention. You can still access archived profiles, however, by clicking the Archived link in the Profiles box. From the Archived page, you can choose to unarchive a profile or delete it from the Profile Organizer.

This chapter introduces you to the many tools that enable access to LinkedIn data from other websites and software.

8

Saving Time with LinkedIn Tools

As a LinkedIn member, you want to maximize the value you receive from the site. Integrating the vast amount of data on LinkedIn with other applications such as browsers, popular websites, and email clients is one of the best ways to do that.

In this chapter, you learn about LinkedIn's many tools, including those that integrate with Firefox, Internet Explorer, Outlook, and Lotus Notes. You can also listen to tips on getting the most from these integration tools and watch videos that show you how to install the LinkedIn Firefox Browser toolbar, use JobsInsider to enhance your job search, and create an email signature.

Understanding LinkedIn Tools

LinkedIn offers several tools, toolbars, and widgets that enhance your LinkedIn experience, both on and off the site. Options include the following:

- **Browser Toolbar.** Search and access LinkedIn data from Firefox or Internet Explorer.

- **JobsInsider.** Discover members of your LinkedIn network who work at companies whose job postings you're viewing. This includes the Browser toolbar.

- **Outlook Toolbar.** Manage your LinkedIn network from Microsoft Outlook.

- **Email Signature.** Create a customized email signature from your profile data to use with popular email systems.

- **Google Toolbar Assistant.** Add a LinkedIn Search button to the Google toolbar.

- **Mac Search Widget.** Search LinkedIn from your Mac Dashboard.

- **Mobile.** Access your LinkedIn network via mobile devices. See Chapter 18, "Accessing LinkedIn via Mobile Devices," for more information.

- **LinkedIn Widget for Lotus Notes.** Integrate your LinkedIn content with Lotus Notes.

TELL ME MORE   Media 8.1—LinkedIn Tools

Access this audio recording through your registered Web edition at
my.safaribooksonline.com/9780789745095/media.

You can access LinkedIn tools from the Tools row on the bottom navigation menu
of the LinkedIn home page.

Installing and Using the LinkedIn Firefox Browser Toolbar

The LinkedIn Firefox Browser Toolbar, also called the LinkedIn Companion for Firefox, is available for a PC or Mac running Firefox versions 2.0 or 3.0. System requirements include Windows XP/Vista or Mac OS X 10.2 or later.

Another option for Mac users is the Mac Search Widget, which enables you to
search LinkedIn from your Mac Dashboard. The widget requires OS 10.4. To
download the widget, click the Tools link on the bottom navigation menu and
then click the Download It Now button in the Mac Search Widget section.

 SHOW ME   Media 8.2—Installing the LinkedIn Firefox Browser Toolbar

Access this video file through your registered Web edition at
my.safaribooksonline.com/9780789745095/media.

 LET ME TRY IT

Installing the LinkedIn Firefox Browser Toolbar

To install the LinkedIn Firefox Browser Toolbar, follow these steps:

1. Click the Tools link on the bottom navigation menu.

2. In the Browser Toolbar box (see Figure 8.1), hover your mouse over the
    Download It Now button and select Firefox (Macintosh and PC) from the
    drop-down menu.

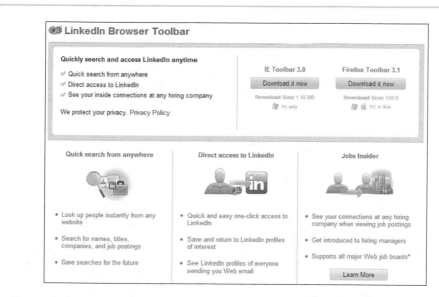

Figure 8.1   *Download the Firefox Browser Toolbar to search and access LinkedIn from your browser.*

If you have concerns about installing and using the toolbar, click the Learn More button and then click the Privacy Policy link to learn exactly how LinkedIn uses your personal data with this tool.

3. Click the OK button to confirm that you are located in one of the countries listed in the pop-up box (depending on your system, this might not appear). In addition, Firefox might try to prevent you from installing the toolbar. If you receive a warning message, click the Allow button to continue installation.

4. Click the Install Now button in the window that appears.

5. Restart Firefox to complete your changes.

Using the LinkedIn Firefox Browser Toolbar

The toolbar now appears in Firefox (see Figure 8.2).

If the LinkedIn buttons don't appear on your browser toolbar, try one of the following:

- Verify that you meet all the listed system requirements.

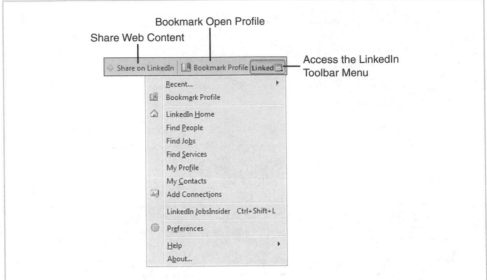

Figure 8.2   *Use the LinkedIn Firefox Browser toolbar to locate and share information on LinkedIn.*

- Click the View menu, click Toolbars, and then click Bookmarks Toolbar to display the Bookmarks toolbar on Firefox.

- Click the View menu, click Toolbars, and then click Customize. In the Customize Toolbars dialog box, select Icons and Text from the Show drop-down list, drag the LinkedIn icon to the toolbar, and click the Done button.

Click the LinkedIn button on your browser toolbar to display a drop-down list of options. These include the following:

- **Recent.** Displays links to your recent profile, recent searches, and job page views. To clear this data, click the Remove options.

- **Bookmark Profile.** Lets you create a Firefox bookmark for an active LinkedIn page. This option is available only if you're viewing a LinkedIn page that you can bookmark, such as a profile, search results, or a job listing. The Bookmark Profile button also appears on the toolbar if this feature is available.

- **LinkedIn Home.** Takes you to LinkedIn's home page. This section also includes direct links to Find People, Find Jobs, Find Services, My Profile, My Contacts, and Add Connections.

- **LinkedIn JobsInsider.** Opens the LinkedIn JobsInsider window. See the "Using the JobsInsider" section later in this chapter for more information.

- **Preferences.** Opens the Preferences dialog box, shown in Figure 8.3, where you can enter your LinkedIn account information, specify how much information to show on the Recent menu, specify when to open the JobsInsider, and activate the InfoBox in Web email option.

- **Help.** Opens a help file where you can search for more information.
- **About.** Displays information about the toolbar.

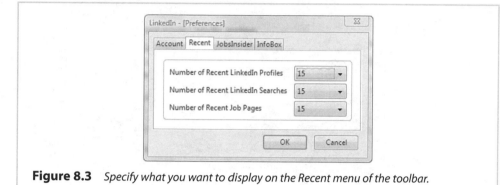

Figure 8.3   *Specify what you want to display on the Recent menu of the toolbar.*

To uninstall the toolbar, select Tools, Add-Ons from the Firefox menu and click the Uninstall button in the LinkedIn Companion for Firefox section.

Sharing Web Pages with LinkedIn Members

You can easily share news stories, blog posts, and other interesting Web content with LinkedIn members, including your connections and fellow members of groups.

 LET ME TRY IT

Sharing Web Pages

To share Web pages, follow these steps:

1. In Firefox, navigate to the page you want to share.

2. Click the Share on LinkedIn button on the toolbar.

3. In the pop-up box that opens (see Figure 8.4), select the LinkedIn members with whom you want to share this content. Options include your connections or the members of any group to which you belong.

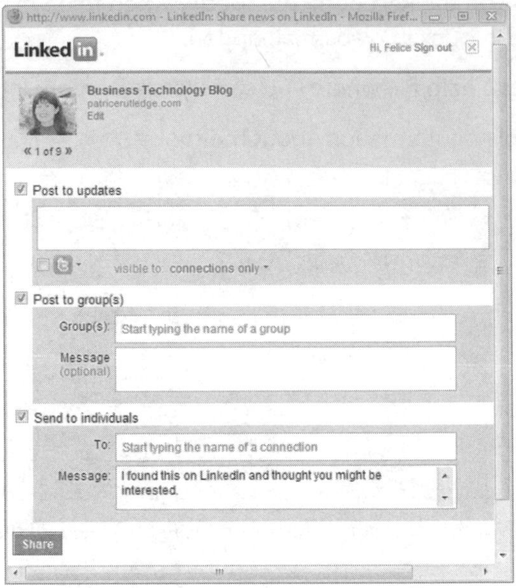

Figure 8.4   *Share selected Web pages with LinkedIn connections or group members.*

4. Click the Share button to share with other LinkedIn members.

Although the Share on LinkedIn button provides a convenient way to share content on LinkedIn, it's a powerful tool that you shouldn't overuse. To generate a positive response from other LinkedIn members, focus on sharing only the most useful, relevant content that affects the majority of group members. For example, share a top news story or an insightful report that affects your industry. Don't share promotional material, sales pages, or your daily blog posts (unless one contains highly useful or relevant content).

Installing and Using the LinkedIn Internet Explorer Toolbar

The LinkedIn Internet Explorer Toolbar is available for the PC only, running Microsoft Windows 2000/XP, with Microsoft Internet Explorer 6.0 and 7.0.

 **LET ME TRY IT**

Installing the LinkedIn Internet Explorer Toolbar

To install the LinkedIn Internet Explorer Toolbar, follow these steps:

1. Click the Tools link on the bottom navigation menu.

2. In the Browser Toolbar box (refer to Figure 8.1), hover your mouse over the Download It Now button and select Internet Explorer (PC Only) from the drop-down menu.

3. Click the OK button to confirm that you are located in one of the countries listed in the pop-up box (depending on your system, this might not appear).

4. Click the Run button. The LinkedIn Internet Explorer Toolbar Setup dialog box appears, shown in Figure 8.5.

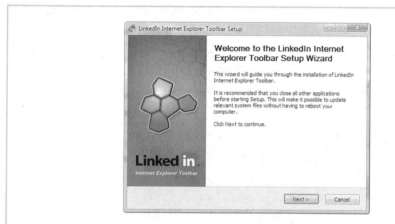

Figure 8.5   *Setting up the LinkedIn Internet Explorer Toolbar.*

5. Click the Next button to continue.

6. Select the checkbox to accept the license agreement and click the Next button.

7. Accept the default installation folder and click the Install button. Alternatively, click the Browse button to select another folder.

8. A warning dialog box prompts you to close all open Internet Explorer windows. Do so, and click the Yes button to continue.

9. Select the Launch Internet Explorer with LinkedIn Toolbar checkbox and click the Finish button.

Internet Explorer opens with the toolbar installed, shown in Figure 8.6.

Figure 8.6   *Search, access, and bookmark pages from LinkedIn while using Internet Explorer.*

If the LinkedIn toolbar doesn't appear, select View, Toolbars, LinkedIn Toolbar from the browser menu. If this menu doesn't appear, right-click and select Menu Bar.

Click the down arrow to the right of the LinkedIn button on your browser toolbar to display a drop-down list of options. These include the following:

- **LinkedIn Home.** Takes you to LinkedIn's home page. This section also includes direct links to Find People, Find Jobs, Find Services, My Profile, and My Contacts.

- **Preferences.** Opens the Preferences dialog box, shown in Figure 8.7, where you can enter your LinkedIn account information, specify when to open the JobsInsider, and activate the InfoBox in Web email option.

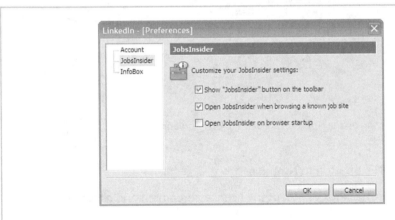

Figure 8.7   *Specify your JobsInsider preferences in this dialog box.*

- **Help.** Opens a help file where you can search for more information.

- **Check for Update.** Checks to see whether there is a more recent version of the toolbar.

- **About.** Displays information about the toolbar.

The LinkedIn Toolbar also includes the following buttons:

- **Search.** Click the down arrow to the right of the Search button to select search options. Options include all keywords, name, title, current title, company, current company, and jobs. Enter your search term and click the Search button to display relevant results in LinkedIn. You can also select the Clear Search History menu to clear your searches or the Advanced Search option to open the Advanced Search page in LinkedIn.

- **Bookmarks.** Click the Bookmark This Profile menu option to bookmark an active LinkedIn page. This option is available only if you're viewing a LinkedIn page that you can bookmark, such as a profile, search results, or a job listing. Select the Manage Bookmarks to open the Bookmarks window.

- **JobsInsider.** Opens the JobsInsider window. See the "Installing and Using JobsInsider" section later in this chapter for more information.

To remove the LinkedIn Internet Explorer toolbar, select Start, Control Panel, Add or Remove Programs and then click the Change/Remove button in the LinkedIn Internet Explorer Toolbar section.

Installing and Using JobsInsider

LinkedIn JobsInsider is a LinkedIn Browser Toolbar feature that assists in your job search. When you're viewing a job posting, JobsInsider lets you know about LinkedIn members in your network who work at that company and are potential inside connections for you. JobsInsider works with job postings on sites such as Monster, CareerBuilder, HotJobs, Craigslist, Simply Hired, Dice, or Vault.

If you haven't installed the LinkedIn Browser Toolbar yet, click the JobsInsider link on the bottom navigation menu for installation instructions. See the "Installing and Using the LinkedIn Firefox Browser Toolbar" section earlier in this chapter for more information.

For example, if you're searching Monster.com for potential jobs, JobsInsider opens automatically, detecting that you're searching a job site. Figure 8.8 shows a sample view of JobsInsider.

When you open a job posting, JobsInsider lists the names of your 1st-degree connections and includes links to their LinkedIn profiles. It also tells you the total people in your network who work at this company. Click the number to view a list of these people.

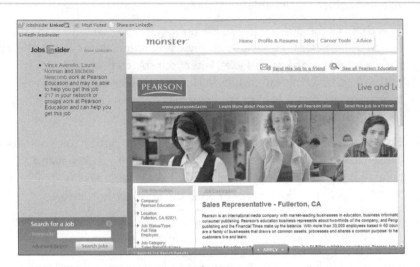

Figure 8.8   *JobsInsider points out your inside connections at a hiring company.*

To specify JobsInsider settings, click the LinkedIn button on your browser tool-bar and select Preferences from the menu. In the Preferences dialog box, you can specify if you want to open JobsInsider when browsing a known job site, open upon browser startup, or not open at all.

Installing and Using the Outlook Toolbar

With the Outlook Toolbar, you can manage your LinkedIn network from within Microsoft Outlook. The toolbar requires that you're running Windows XP or Vista and using Microsoft Outlook XP (2002), 2003, or 2007.

 **LET ME TRY IT**

Installing the Outlook Toolbar

To install the Outlook Toolbar, follow these steps:

1.   Click the Tools link on the bottom navigation menu.

2.   In the Outlook Toolbar box (refer to Figure 8.1), click the Download It Now button.

3.   Click the OK button to confirm that you are located in one of the countries listed in the pop-up box.

4. Click Run to run the file. The LinkedIn Outlook Toolbar Setup dialog box opens.

5. Click the Next button to continue.

6. Select the checkbox to accept the license agreement and click the Next button.

7. Accept the default installation folder and click the Install button. Alternatively, click the Browse button to select another folder.

8. Select the Launch Microsoft Outlook with LinkedIn Outlook Toolbar checkbox and click the Finish button.

The LinkedIn toolbar and menu now appear in Outlook. The toolbar enables you to do the following:

- Receive suggestions about who to connect with on LinkedIn based on email frequency

- Send LinkedIn invitations with one click

- Update Outlook based on LinkedIn profile data

- Get notified when your contacts update their LinkedIn profiles

- Stay current with your network using the LinkedIn dashboard

- Search and access LinkedIn data from Outlook

Creating LinkedIn Email Signatures

LinkedIn enables you to create an email signature that includes links to your profile and other popular LinkedIn features.

The LinkedIn email signature works with the following:

- Outlook 2000, XP, 2003, or 2007

- Outlook Express

- Mozilla Thunderbird

- Yahoo! Mail (using the "Simple - Plain" layout with Internet Explorer 5.5 or later on Windows)

 SHOW ME   Media 8.3—Creating an Email Signature
Access this video file through your registered Web edition at
my.safaribooksonline.com/9780789745095/media.

LET ME TRY IT

Creating an Email Signature

To create an email signature, follow these steps:

1. Click the Tools link on the bottom navigation menu of the LinkedIn home page.

2. In the Email Signature section of the LinkedIn Tools page, click the Try It Now button. The Create Email Signature page opens, shown in Figure 8.9.

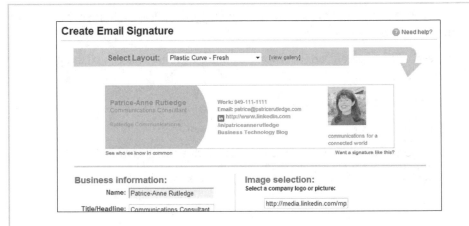

Figure 8.9 *Create an email signature you can use with many popular email systems.*

3. Select a layout for your email signature from the drop-down list. A preview of your signature with the selected layout appears on the page. To view all the options at once, click the View Gallery link.

4. Enter the contact information you want to appear on your signature in the Business Information, Contact Information, and Work Address sections.

5. If you want to include a company logo or your photo, enter the image's URL in the Image Selection field. Your image must be in the GIF, JPG, or PNG format; no larger than 50k; and no larger than 100 X 60 in size. To use your LinkedIn photo, right-click the photo on your profile and choose Copy Image Location or Copy Shortcut from the menu. (The menu option varies by browser.) Paste (Ctrl+V) this link in the Image Selection field.

You must link to an image that already appears on the Web, such as your LinkedIn photo or an image on your own website or blog. You can't upload an image.

6. Select any or all of the following options to place links on your email sig-
    nature:

    - Professional Profile link
    - See Who We Know in Common link
    - We're Hiring link

7. Click the Click Here for Instructions link to save your signature. A new win-
    dow opens, shown in Figure 8.10.

Figure 8.10   *Copy and paste the code for your new email signature into your email system.*

8. Copy your signature code by clicking in the text box and pressing Ctrl + C
    on your keyboard.

9. Select your email client from the drop-down list. Instructions for using the
    email signature in your email system appear.

10. Click the Close This Window link to close the window.

11. Go to your email program to complete the installation of your new email sig-
    nature.

Installing and Using the Google Toolbar Assistant

The Google Toolbar Assistant optimizes the Google Toolbar by installing a LinkedIn Search button. You must have installed the Google Toolbar (http://toolbar.google.com) for Firefox or Internet Explorer to use this feature.

 LET ME TRY IT

Installing the Google Toolbar Assistant

To install the Google Toolbar Assistant, follow these steps:

1. Click the Tools link on the bottom navigation menu.

2. In the Google Toolbar Assistant section of the LinkedIn Tools page, click the Download It Now button. The Google Toolbar Custom Button Installer dialog box opens. If you haven't installed the Google Toolbar yet, you're prompted to do so before continuing.

3. Click the Add button.

4. In the dialog box that opens, specify whether you want to search by keywords or name in the Search Method field. You can change this later (see Figure 8.11).

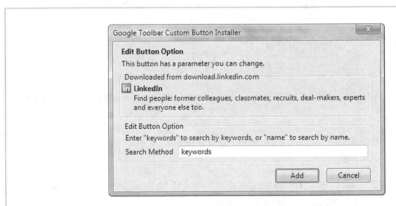

Figure 8.11   *Specify a search method for the LinkedIn button on the Google Toolbar.*

5. Click the OK button. LinkedIn places the LinkedIn Search button on the Google Toolbar (see Figure 8.12).

To use the Search button, enter a search term in the text box and click the LinkedIn button. LinkedIn displays results based on the type of search method you specified (either a keyword or a name).

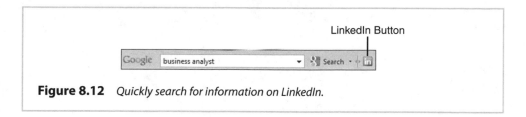

Figure 8.12   *Quickly search for information on LinkedIn.*

To change your search method or remove the Search button, right-click the LinkedIn button and select LinkedIn Button Options from the menu.

This chapter teaches you how to use LinkedIn as an effective job search tool.

9

Searching for Jobs

LinkedIn offers many powerful tools for job seekers, including a comprehensive jobs database, profiles of thousands of recruiters and hiring managers, detailed company information, the JobsInsider toolbar, and much more.

In this chapter, you explore the many ways LinkedIn can help you in your job search. You can also listen to tips on attracting the right attention as a job seeker and watch videos that show you how to search for jobs, perform an advanced job search, and search for recruiters and hiring managers.

Attracting Recruiters and Hiring Managers

LinkedIn is an excellent tool for job seekers, but you need to create a stellar profile and develop a solid network if you want to maximize your results. Here are several tips for making the most of LinkedIn as a job search tool:

- **Complete your profile.** LinkedIn reports that members with a complete profile generate 40 times more opportunities than those whose profiles aren't complete.

- **Develop a solid network of connections.** Your ability to use job search features such as JobsInsider or Inside Connections depends on having a reasonable number of connections. You should aim for at least 50 connections to maximize the benefits of these features, although they do work with fewer connections.

- **Get recommendations.** A complete profile includes at least three recommendations. Aim for recommendations from managers, executives, or actual clients. Peer recommendations, particularly those that you "trade" with colleagues by recommending each other, carry far less weight.

- **Include keywords that are relevant to your profession and industry, such as skills, certifications, and degrees.** Recruiters search for these words, and your profile should include them if you want to be found.

- **Focus on results, not a list of duties.** Remember that your profile is a concise summary of your qualifications, not a resume (although you can attach one if you like). Emphasize your results and accomplishments; don't just list tasks you performed.

- **Post a resume or portfolio.** Using LinkedIn applications such as Box.net files, you can attach PDFs to your profile.

- **Indicate on your profile that you're seeking employment.** If you're unemployed, include this information in your status, professional headline, or summary. Don't sound desperate, but do let your network know that you're looking for opportunities.

 TELL ME MORE   Media 9.1—Attracting Recruiters and Hiring Managers

Access this audio recording through your registered Web Edition at my.safaribooksonline.com/9780789745095/media.

See Chapter 2, "Creating Your LinkedIn Profile," and Chapter 10, "Managing LinkedIn Recommendations," for more information.

Keep in mind that many recruiters now search the Web for background information on potential candidates. It isn't enough to have a professional presence on LinkedIn. Review any other social networking profiles you have to ensure they also reinforce your professional image. If not, remove your "digital dirt" before you begin your job search.

Searching Job Postings

LinkedIn offers a large database of job postings that are posted directly on LinkedIn as well as on its partner site, Simply Hired.

Although the Jobs page is LinkedIn's primary job search tool, you should also search the Jobs Discussion Board for any group you belong to, as well as the Jobs box on the company profiles for your target employers. To do a quick search for jobs, use the search box on the global navigation bar.

SHOW ME   Media 9.2—Searching Job Postings
Access this video file through your registered Web Edition at
my.safaribooksonline.com/9780789745095/media.

 LET ME TRY IT

Searching for a Job

To search job postings on LinkedIn, follow these steps:

1. On the global navigation bar, click the Jobs link. The Jobs page opens, shown in Figure 9.1.

Figure 9.1   *Searching for jobs by keyword.*

2. Enter keywords related to your job search. For example, you could enter a job title, a job skill, or the name of a target company.

3. Click the Search button. The Job Search Results page opens, shown in Figure 9.2.

On this page, you can do the following:

- Sort jobs by relevance, your relationship to the job poster, or the date posted (most recent or earliest).

- Identify the company by its logo (not available for all postings).

- Open the job posting by clicking the job title link.

- Click the Find People in Your Network link to display a list of people in your network who work for this company.

- Refine your search criteria using the fields on the left side of the page. The fields in the Job Search box are nearly identical to the fields on the Advanced Job Search page. See "Using Advanced Job Search Techniques," later in this chapter, for more information.

Figure 9.2   *Viewing a list of jobs that match your criteria.*

Viewing Job Postings

The content listed on a job posting varies according to what the hiring company chooses to display. The content that you see will also vary according to what type of connection you have to the poster and the connections you have to the people working at that company. A job posting (see Figure 9.3) might include some or all of the following features:

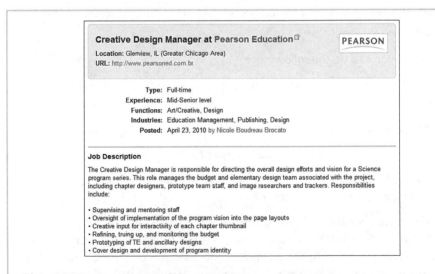

Figure 9.3   *Viewing a list of jobs that match sample criteria.*

- A header listing the job title, location, and company URL.

- A detailed job description.

- The Apply Now button. Click this button to apply for the job from LinkedIn. See the "Applying for a Job" section later in this chapter for more information. Alternatively, the Apply on Company Website button might display if a company prefers to use its own application process.

- The Forward Job link. Click to send a message to a connection who might be interested in this job.

- The Follow Company link, which enables you to follow this company's activity on LinkedIn.

- The Request Referral button. Click this button to open the Introductions page where you can request an introduction to the job poster. You can request introductions only to job posters in your network. Otherwise, the Request Referral button doesn't appear. See Chapter 6, "Communicating with Your LinkedIn Network," for more information about LinkedIn introductions.

- The Posted By Box with a link to the job poster's LinkedIn profile. A connection icon appears if this person is in your network. For example, if a job poster is connected to one of your connections, the 2nd-degree connection icon appears.

- The You're Linked to [Company Name] box. This box lists LinkedIn members in your network who work at this company. These people could provide you with inside information about potential job opportunities at the company.

Using Advanced Job Search Techniques

If you want to search for jobs based on specific criteria, try an advanced job search.

SHOW ME   Media 9.3—Performing an Advanced Job Search
Access this video file through your registered Web Edition at
my.safaribooksonline.com/9780789745095/media.

 **LET ME TRY IT**

Performing an Advanced Job Search

To perform an advanced job search, follow these steps:

1. On the global navigation bar, click the Jobs link.

2. Click the Advanced Search tab to open the Advanced Job Search page, shown in Figure 9.4.

Figure 9.4 *Performing an advanced job search.*

3. In the Keywords text box, enter keywords (such as a job title, a skill, or a certification). See Chapter 7, "Searching for People on LinkedIn," for more information on using advanced search criteria.

4. Specify the criteria for your search. Options include the following:
    - Location
    - Job Title
    - Company
    - Functions (such as Accounting/Auditing, Engineering, Finance, Information Technology, Marketing, and so on)
    - Industries (such as Banking, Biotechnology, Computer Software, Insurance, Real Estate, and so on)
    - Experience (ranging from executive jobs to internships)
    - When Posted (the date the job was posted, such as in the last day or at any time)
    - Sort By (specific criteria such as date posted or relevance to your keywords)

5. Click the Search button to display job search results.

See the previous section, "Searching Job Postings," for more information about the Job Search Results page.

You don't need to specify criteria in all the fields available on the Advanced Search page. Start with a few choices and then narrow or expand your search based on your search results.

Applying for Jobs

LinkedIn offers two ways to apply for jobs, based on the way the company posting a job handles its recruitment. If the Apply on Company Website button displays on a job posting, clicking this button takes you to the company's external website, where you can apply for the job. If the Apply Now button displays on the job posting, clicking this button directs you to a job application form on LinkedIn. In this section, you learn how to complete LinkedIn's own job application form.

 LET ME TRY IT

Applying for a Job on LinkedIn

You can apply for a job posted on LinkedIn directly from the job posting. To do so, follow these steps:

1. In the job description for the job you would like to apply for, click the Apply Now button to open an application page. Figure 9.5 shows a sample application page.

2. In the Contact Information section, enter details about your name, email address, and contact information.

3. In the Cover Letter and Resume section, enter your cover letter. A good cover letter summarizes strengths and accomplishments that are relevant to this job and is personalized for this target job.

4. Click the Browse button next to the Resume field to upload your resume as a text file, Word document, PDF, or HTML file of no more than 200k. LinkedIn attaches your uploaded resume in its original format.

5. Click the Continue button.

6. Review and confirm your application one more time before submitting. Be sure to check for spelling, grammar, and content.

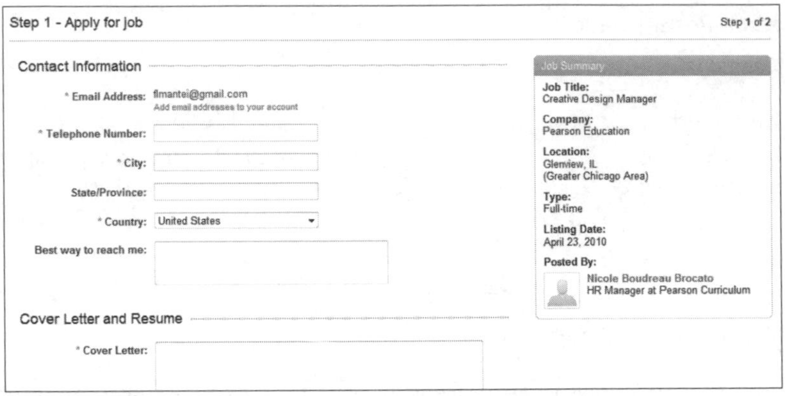

Step 1 - Apply for job   Step 1 of 2

Contact Information

* Email Address: flmantel@gmail.com
                 Add email addresses to your account

* Telephone Number:

* City:

State/Province:

* Country: United States

Best way to reach me:

Cover Letter and Resume

* Cover Letter:

Job Summary

Job Title:
Creative Design Manager

Company:
Pearson Education

Location:
Glenview, IL
(Greater Chicago Area)

Type:
Full-time

Listing Date:
April 23, 2010

Posted By:
Nicole Boudreau Brocato
HR Manager at Pearson Curriculum

Figure 9.5   *Applying for jobs directly from LinkedIn.*

7. Click the Apply Now button to submit your application for the job.

Finding Recruiters and Hiring Managers

SHOW ME   **Media 9.4—Searching for Recruiters and Hiring Managers on LinkedIn**
Access this video file through your registered Web Edition at my.safaribooksonline.com/9780789745095/media.

The good news for job seekers: Thousands of recruiters and hiring managers maintain profiles on LinkedIn. To find them, select People in the quick search box on the global navigation bar. Then click the Advanced link to the right of the box to open the Advanced People Search page, shown in Figure 9.6.

There are several ways to find recruiters and hiring managers on the Advanced People Search page. The following are some examples:

- In the Industries field, select Staffing and Recruiting and enter keywords related to the type of job you're looking for. If applicable, enter location criteria.

- Enter **Recruiter** in the Title field and the name of a company you want to work for.

- Enter **Recruiter** in the Title field and any relevant location information.

Searching for appropriate contacts is a combination of art and science, so you might need to revise your search criteria several times before you find the appropriate people.

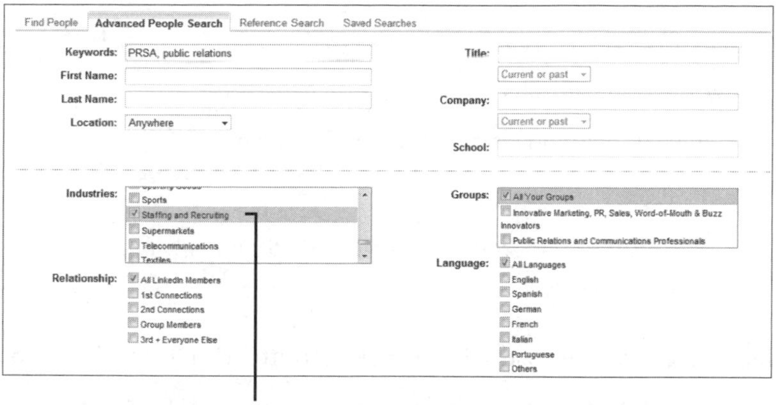

Searching for People in the Staffing and Recruiting Industry

Figure 9.6   *Searching for recruiters and hiring managers on LinkedIn.*

Remember that LinkedIn is a networking and research tool, not a means of spamming prospective recruiters and employers. When you do find good targets for your job search, review their profiles carefully to determine the best way to contact them. Some recruiters provide links to external sites for job candidates. If your target is a hiring manager, determine whether you can reach this person through a network introduction. Alternatively, consider sending a brief message to hiring managers who indicate that they are open to job inquiries.

Upgrading to a Job Seeker Premium Account

LinkedIn offers many free features and opportunities for job seekers. If you need access to LinkedIn premium features to aid in your job search, however, consider upgrading to a Job Seeker premium account. For example, these accounts can provide access to InMail, the Profile Organizer, and the OpenLink Network and increase your available introductions.

All Job Seeker premium accounts enable you to

- Receive placement as a featured applicant when you apply for a job
- Use premium search features
- View who is interested in your profile
- Participate in the OpenLink Network (described in Chapter 1)
- Receive priority customer service from LinkedIn

The Basic account costs US $19.95 per month. With this account, you can

- Create five Profile Organizer folders
- View 100 profile results per search
- Maintain 10 pending introductions at one time

Note that the Basic account doesn't enable you to send any InMail.

The Job Seeker account costs US $29.95 per month. With this account, you can

- Send five InMails per month
- Create 10 Profile Organizer folders
- View 250 profile results per search
- Maintain 15 pending introductions at one time

The Job Seeker Plus account is priced at US $49.95 per month. With this account, you can

- Send 10 InMails per month
- Create 25 Profile Organizer folders
- View 500 profile results per search
- Maintain 25 pending introductions at one time

To upgrade to a Job Seeker Premium account or learn more about upgrade options, select Job Seeker Premium from the Jobs drop-down menu on the global navigation bar.

This chapter shows you how to request and provide professional recommendations on LinkedIn.

10

Managing LinkedIn Recommendations

LinkedIn enables you to request recommendations from and provide recommendations to the people in your professional network. Recommendations are a powerful networking tool, so consider carefully whom you want to ask for a recommendation and whom you want to recommend as part of your overall LinkedIn strategy.

In this chapter, you learn how to request, provide, manage, and revise recommendations. You can also listen to tips on maximizing the power of LinkedIn recommendations and watch videos that show you how to request recommendations, respond to recommendation requests, and make recommendations.

Understanding LinkedIn Recommendations

LinkedIn offers four types of recommendations:

- **Colleague.** You worked with this person at the same company as a manager, peer, or employee.

- **Business Partner.** You worked with this person in another capacity, not as a colleague or client. For example, you worked at partner companies, performed volunteer or association work together, and so forth.

- **Student.** You were a teacher, advisor, or fellow student at the same school.

- **Service Provider.** You hired this person to perform services. Service Provider recommendations differ from the other recommendation types in that they also appear in the LinkedIn Service Providers directory. See Chapter 15, "Using LinkedIn Service Providers," for more information about service provider recommendations.

 TELL ME MORE   Media 10.1—LinkedIn Recommendations

Access this audio recording through your registered Web Edition at
my.safaribooksonline.com/9780789745095/media.

The recommendation process involves several steps between two people to ensure that both approve the recommendation before it is final. For example, if Drake wants to request a recommendation from his former manager, Bianca—a common type of request—the process requires four steps:

- **Step 1.** Drake sends a recommendation request to Bianca.
- **Step 2.** Bianca receives the request and submits a recommendation for Drake.
- **Step 3.** Drake receives a notification about Bianca's recommendation and accepts the recommendation.
- **Step 4.** LinkedIn displays the recommendation on Drake's profile.

Obviously, this process assumes that both Drake and Bianca approve each step. LinkedIn also offers options for you to request clarifications and changes. If you write an unsolicited recommendation for a connection without receiving a recommendation request, your process starts at Step 2 with submitting the recommendation.

Requesting Recommendations

Receiving recommendations from managers, colleagues, and clients can help you achieve your networking goals on LinkedIn. LinkedIn suggests that a complete profile should include at least three recommendations for maximum effectiveness.

Before you send your requests, however, think about what you want to achieve. Be clear about your goals so that your connections write recommendations that help you achieve them. For example, if you want to move into a management position, you should request a recommendation that discusses your leadership abilities. If you want to change careers, emphasize crossover skills.

Although LinkedIn notifies your connections that you've requested a recommendation, it's a good idea that this message doesn't come as a surprise. Talk to the people you want to recommend you so that they're aware of your request and know what to emphasize in their recommendation.

 SHOW ME   Media 10.2—Requesting Recommendations on LinkedIn
Access this video file through your registered Web Edition at
my.safaribooksonline.com/9780789745095/media.

 **LET ME TRY IT**

Requesting a Recommendation

To request a recommendation from one of your connections, follow these steps:

1. On the global navigation bar, select Recommendations from the Profile drop-down menu. The Received Recommendations page opens, shown in Figure 10.1.

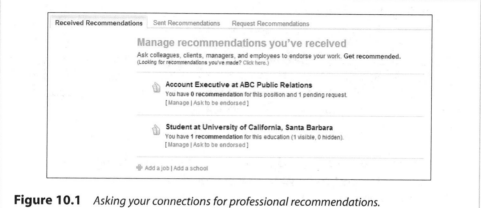

Received Recommendations   Sent Recommendations   Request Recommendations

Manage recommendations you've received

Ask colleagues, clients, managers, and employees to endorse your work. **Get recommended.**
(Looking for recommendations you've made? Click here.)

Account Executive at ABC Public Relations
You have **0 recommendation** for this position and 1 pending request.
[Manage | Ask to be endorsed]

Student at University of California, Santa Barbara
You have **1 recommendation** for this education (1 visible, 0 hidden).
[Manage | Ask to be endorsed]

⊕ Add a job | Add a school

Figure 10.1   *Asking your connections for professional recommendations.*

2. Click the Ask to Be Endorsed link next to the related position or school. The Request Recommendations page opens, shown in Figure 10.2.

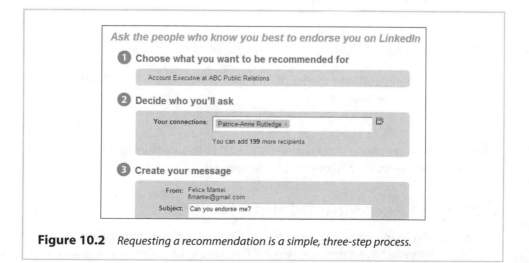

Ask the people who know you best to endorse you on LinkedIn

① **Choose what you want to be recommended for**

Account Executive at ABC Public Relations

② **Decide who you'll ask**

Your connections: Patrice-Anne Rutledge x

You can add **199** more recipients

③ **Create your message**

From: Felice Mantei
flmantei@gmail.com
Subject: Can you endorse me?

Figure 10.2   *Requesting a recommendation is a simple, three-step process.*

> The Received Recommendations page displays only positions and schools you've already entered on your profile. If you haven't done this, click the Add a Job or Add a School link to complete this step first.

3. In Step 1, the position or school you selected appears by default. To change this, return to the previous page.

4. In Step 2, start typing the name of the connection you want to ask for a recommendation. Select the correct name from the drop-down list of options that appear.

> Although you can request a recommendation from up to 200 connections at a time, it's a much better practice to personalize each recommendation request you send. If you really want to send your request to more than one person, however, click the View All Connections icon to select your recipients.

5. In Step 3, create your message asking for a recommendation. LinkedIn provides sample text for you, but you should customize this for each request. Be specific and let your connection know what you want to achieve with this recommendation. You don't need to add a salutation; LinkedIn does this automatically.

6. Click the Send button. LinkedIn sends your recommendation request to its target recipient. If you selected more than one person in Step 2, each person receives an individual message.

> You can also request a recommendation on the Edit My Profile page. To do so, click the Request Recommendations link below the related position or school in the Experience or Education section. If you already have one recommendation, this link is called the Manage link.

See "Responding to Recommendation Requests" to learn what happens when a connection receives your recommendation request.

Managing Recommendation Requests

After you send a recommendation request, the Received Recommendations tab indicates that you have a pending request (see Figure 10.3). This text remains until your connection submits a recommendation for you.

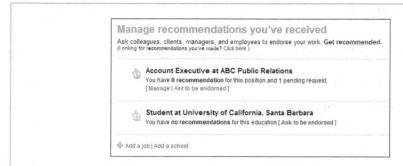

Figure 10.3   *Monitoring your pending recommendation requests.*

To review your request, click the Manage link below the related position or school. The Manage Received Recommendations page opens, shown in Figure 10.4.

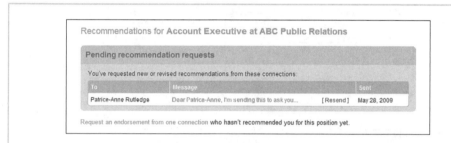

Figure 10.4   *Resend requests that have been pending for more than a week.*

On this page, you can view a list of the recommendations you've requested as well as the date you requested them. If your request has been pending for more than a week, click the Resend link to send your request again with a message to the recipient. It's also a good idea to contact this person directly.

Responding to Recommendation Requests

LinkedIn sends a message to your Inbox when you receive recommendation requests. The default subject line for these messages is "Can You Endorse Me?" unless the person requesting the recommendation modified this text.

SHOW ME   **Media 10.3—Responding to Recommendation Requests on LinkedIn**
Access this video file through your registered Web Edition at
my.safaribooksonline.com/9780789745095/media.

LET ME TRY IT

Responding to a Recommendation Request

To respond to a recommendation request, follow these steps:

1. On the global navigation bar, click the Inbox link. See Chapter 6, "Communicating with Your LinkedIn Network," for more information about working with your Inbox.

2. Select the message that contains the recommendation request. Figure 10.5 illustrates a sample recommendation request.

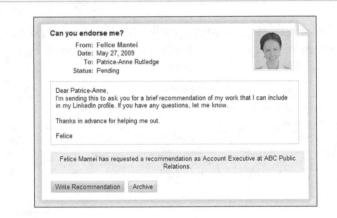

Figure 10.5   *LinkedIn notifies you every time you receive a recommendation request.*

3. Click the Write Recommendation button to write your recommendation. The Select Type page opens, as shown in Figure 10.6.

Figure 10.6   *Your options vary depending on the recommendation type you choose.*

If this is for a student request, LinkedIn doesn't ask you to select a recommendation type and opens the Create Your Recommendation page directly.

4. If this recommendation is for a position, select from the following options: Colleague, Service Provider, or Business Partner. See "Understanding LinkedIn Recommendations," earlier in this chapter, for more information about these recommendation types.

5. Click the Continue button to open the Create Your Recommendation page, shown in Figure 10.7.

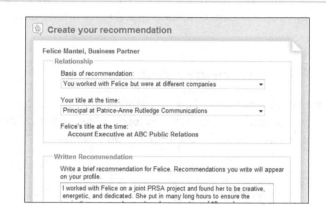

Figure 10.7   *Create a recommendation that describes this person's accomplishments clearly and concisely.*

6. Select a Basis of Recommendation from the drop-down list. Depending on the type of recommendation you're giving, these options could include the following:

    *   **Colleague.** Specify whether you managed this person; reported to this person; were senior to this person, but didn't manage this person directly; held a lower position, but didn't report to this person; worked in the same group; or worked in different groups.
    *   **Business Partner.** Specify whether you worked together at different companies or whether the person was your client.
    *   **Student.** Specify whether you were a teacher, advisor, or fellow student.

7. Select Your Title at the Time from the drop-down list, which includes the positions on your profile.

8. Enter your recommendation in the Written Recommendation box. Write a concise, specific recommendation that relates to the position and the goals of the person you're recommending.

9. Click the View/Edit link to display the Personalize This Message text box, where you can personalize the message you send to the person requesting your recommendation. This text doesn't appear on the recommendation itself.

10. Click the Send button to send the recommendation and accompanying message to the requestor.

Consider carefully before recommending someone on LinkedIn. Remember that your reputation is based not only on who recommends you, but also on who you recommend. Is this someone you would recommend in the real world? If not, reply privately to the person and explain that you don't feel comfortable giving the recommendation. For example, you might not know the person well enough for a recommendation, or your experience working together might not have been a positive one.

Accepting Recommendations

When someone recommends you, LinkedIn sends you a notification message (see Figure 10.8). If you indicate that you want to receive email notifications on the Account & Settings page, LinkedIn also notifies you by email.

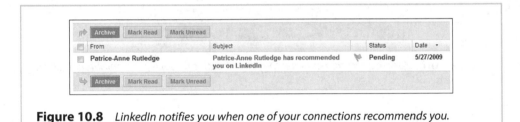

Figure 10.8 *LinkedIn notifies you when one of your connections recommends you.*

Open the message to view the complete recommendation. Figure 10.9 illustrates a sample message.

Figure 10.9 *Review your recommendation for accuracy before accepting it.*

On this page, you can do the following:

- Select Show This Recommendation on My Profile if you want to display the recommendation.

- Select Hide This Recommendation on My Profile if you want to hide the recommendation. In general, displaying your recommendations is a good promotional tool. You should hide unsolicited recommendations you don't want others to view.

- Click the Accept Recommendation button to accept the recommendation.

- Click the Request Replacement button to ask for a revised recommendation. This option is useful if the recommendation isn't accurate, contains misspellings, or doesn't focus on your current goals or accomplishments. To ensure you receive a more appropriate recommendation, be sure to specify why you need a replacement.

If you accept your recommendation and choose to show it on your profile, you can view it below its related position or school (see Figure 10.10).

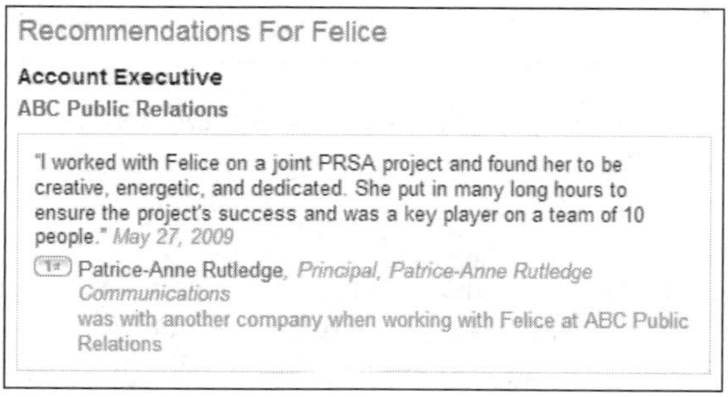

Recommendations For Felice

Account Executive
ABC Public Relations

"I worked with Felice on a joint PRSA project and found her to be creative, energetic, and dedicated. She put in many long hours to ensure the project's success and was a key player on a team of 10 people." *May 27, 2009*

Patrice-Anne Rutledge, *Principal, Patrice-Anne Rutledge Communications*
was with another company when working with Felice at ABC Public Relations

Figure 10.10   *View accepted recommendations on your profile.*

Making Recommendations

At times, you might want to recommend your connections even if they don't send you a recommendation request.

SHOW ME   **Media 10.4—Making Recommendations on LinkedIn**
Access this video file through your registered Web Edition at
my.safaribooksonline.com/9780789745095/media.

LET ME TRY IT

Making a Recommendation

To make a recommendation, follow these steps:

1. On the global navigation bar, select Recommendations from the Profile drop-down menu.

2. Scroll down the Received Recommendations page to the Make a Recommendation box, shown in Figure 10.11.

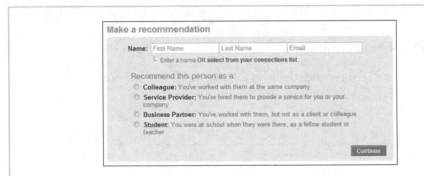

Figure 10.11 *You can make several kinds of recommendations on LinkedIn.*

Another way to initiate a recommendation is to visit a connection's profile page and click the Recommend link below the related position or school, which opens the Create Your Recommendation page. Or, click the Recommend This Person link in the upper-right corner of a connection's LinkedIn profile.

3. Click the Select from Your Connections List link to select your target recipient. Alternatively, enter a person's name and email address.

4. Select the type of recommendation you want to write. Options include Colleague, Service Provider, Business Partner, or Student. See Chapter 15, "Using LinkedIn Service Providers," for more information about service provider recommendations.

5. Click the Continue button to open the Create Your Recommendation page.

See "Responding to Recommendation Requests" earlier in this chapter for more information on completing the Create Your Recommendation page. The process is the same whether you respond to a recommendation request or initiate it yourself.

Managing Recommendations

Several times a year, you should review your recommendations to verify that they're still relevant to your current goals. You might want to hide a recommendation that's no longer relevant or request updated recommendations from those who have recommended you in the past.

To manage your recommendations, select Recommendations from the Profile drop-down menu on the global navigation bar.

Managing Received Recommendations

On the Received Recommendations page, click the Manage link below the recommendation you want to change. The Manage Received Recommendations page opens, shown in Figure 10.12.

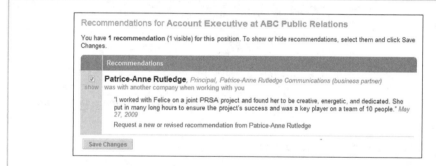

Figure 10.12 *Review your recommendations regularly to verify that they still meet your needs.*

To hide a recommendation from your profile, remove the checkmark next to the Show checkbox. Click the Save Changes button to save this change.

To ask a connection for a revised recommendation, click the Request a New or Revised Recommendation From [Name] link. LinkedIn sends a message to this connection asking for a revision. Be sure to communicate clearly what you're looking for in your revised recommendation. For example, you might want to revise a recommendation if your job duties for the same position have changed or you want to emphasize a different aspect of your job for future career growth.

If you receive a promotion or have a new job title, add a new position and request a recommendation for that job rather than revise an existing recommendation.

Managing Sent Recommendations

To manage the recommendations you give others, select Recommendations from the Profile drop-down menu on the global navigation bar. Click the Sent Recommendations tab to open the Sent Recommendations page, shown in Figure 10.13.

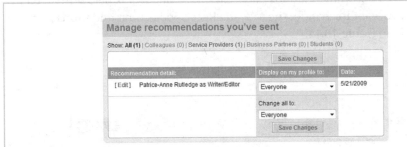

Figure 10.13   *Revise or withdraw a recommendation on the Sent Recommendations page.*

On this page, you can do the following:

- **Change the display options for a recommendation.** By default, the recommendations you give your connections appear on your profile for all LinkedIn members to see. Click the Display on My Profile To drop-down list and choose either Connections Only or No One to change this.

- **Revise a recommendation.** Click the Edit link next to the recommendation you want to revise and make your changes on the Edit Your Recommendation page. Click the Send button to make your changes and notify your connection.

- **Withdraw a recommendation.** Click the Edit link next to the recommendation you want to withdraw. On the Edit Your Recommendation page, click the Withdraw This Recommendation link. A pop-up box asks you to confirm that you want to withdraw the recommendation.

This chapter explores LinkedIn's many options for recruiting top talent.

11

Recruiting Job Candidates

Even in an employer's market, it can be difficult to find the right candidate, particularly for a job that requires specific expertise and experience. Fortunately, LinkedIn offers several ways to attract the top talent among its many millions of members.

In this chapter, you learn how to post jobs, purchase job credits, search for targeted job candidates, and perform reference searches. You can also listen to advice on using LinkedIn as a recruitment tool and watch videos that show you how to post a job and purchase job credits.

Understanding LinkedIn's Recruitment Options

LinkedIn offers numerous options for recruiters, hiring managers, and small businesses to locate and recruit top talent.

On LinkedIn, you can

- Post a job for $195 that's searchable by LinkedIn's millions of members
- Purchase job credits for discounted job postings
- Post a job on a group's Jobs Discussion Board at no cost
- Search for candidates using LinkedIn's advanced search features
- Perform reference searches on potential candidates
- Upgrade to a premium account to send more InMails to potential candidates
- Sign up for LinkedIn Talent Advantage, a corporate recruiting solution for larger companies

Which option is right for you depends on your budget, the size of your company, and the type of candidates you want to attract.

TELL ME MORE   Media 11.1—LinkedIn's Recruitment Options

Access this audio recording through your registered Web Edition at
my.safaribooksonline.com/9780789745095/media.

Posting Jobs on LinkedIn

LinkedIn charges $195 for a 30-day job posting. If you plan to post multiple jobs, you'll save money by purchasing discount job credits. See the "Purchasing Job Credits" section later in this chapter.

SHOW ME   Media 11.2—Posting a Job on LinkedIn

Access this video file through your registered Web Edition at
my.safaribooksonline.com/9780789745095/media.

LET ME TRY IT

Posting a Job

To post a job on LinkedIn, follow these steps:

1. On the global navigation bar, select Post a Job from the Jobs drop-down menu. The Step 1—Job Description page opens, shown in Figure 11.1.

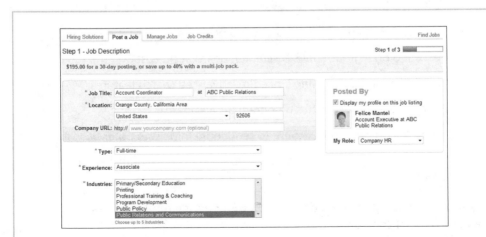

Figure 11.1 *Post a job that could reach LinkedIn's millions of members.*

The Job Description page lists several fields as optional, but you'll get better results with a job posting that contains as much detail as possible. In addition to basic job duties, emphasize the perks and benefits of the position to attract quality candidates.

2. Enter a job title and verify that the text box to the right of this field displays the correct company name. The job poster's current company appears by default, but you can edit this text box.

3. Enter your company's location, including a city/regional area, country, and postal code, if applicable. In addition, enter an optional company URL.

4. In the Posted By box, indicate whether you want to display your profile on the job listing. If so, verify that your title is correct and select your job role, such as hiring manager.

5. In the Type drop-down list, select one of the following: full-time, part-time, contract, temporary, or other.

6. Indicate the experience level of your desired candidate, such as executive, director, mid-senior level, associate, entry level, internship, or not applicable.

7. Select up to five industries and five job functions by holding down the Control (Ctrl) key to make multiple selections.

8. Enter an employer job ID. This can be an internal reference number for your records.

9. Enter optional compensation information including currency, pay range, and any additional information, such as bonus potential, commissions, and so forth. Pay range data can help ensure that candidates in the right pay range apply to your position.

10. Enter optional referral bonus information including currency, payment, and additional information. You can enter more than one referral bonus if your bonus amounts vary based on the referrer. For example, you can create referral bonuses for employees, for non-employees such as temporary workers or contractors, and for the general public (anyone), each with a different bonus amount.

11. Enter a detailed job description of up to 25,000 characters. Candidates search for jobs using keywords. Be sure your post contains the right keywords to attract top candidates. Job skills, certifications, and degrees—such as Java, PMP, CPA, or MBA—are good keywords.

12. Provide optional information about the skills required and a company description. You can enter up to 4,000 characters in each text box.

13. Select the Local Candidates Only, No Relocation checkbox or the Third Party Applications from Staffing Agencies Not Accepted checkbox, if applicable.

> If you want to save your in-progress job posting, click the Save as Draft button. To return to your saved draft, select Manage Jobs from the Jobs drop-down menu on the global navigation bar.

14. Click the Continue button. The Step 2—Options page opens, shown in Figure 11.2.

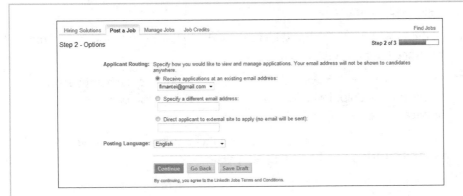

Figure 11.2   *Specify how you want to view and manage applications in Step 2.*

15. In the Applicant Routing field, specify how you want to receive applications. Your options include sending applications to an email address already listed on LinkedIn, sending applications to a different email address, or directing applicants to an external website such as your company's own job listing page.

16. Select a posting language from the drop-down list.

17. Click the Continue button to open the Purchase: Billing Information page. Alternatively, click the Go Back button to return to the previous page or click the Save as Draft button to save your job posting for later.

> Be sure to check your job posting carefully for spelling, grammar, and content errors.

18. Enter your billing information and credit card data (unless you have available job credits), and then click the Buy Now button (see Figure 11.3).

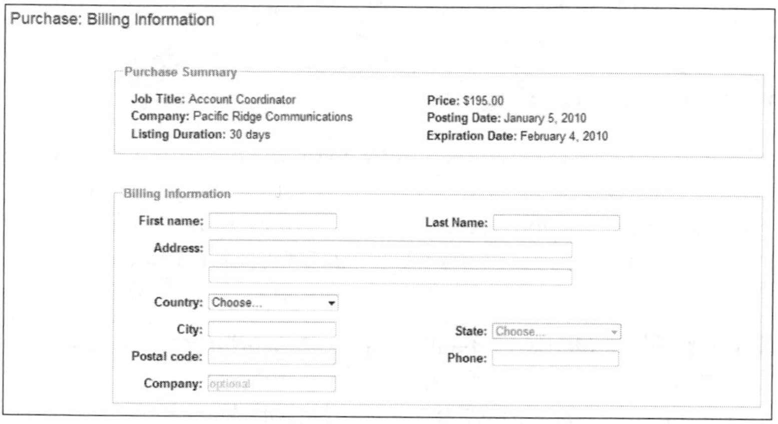

Purchase: Billing Information

Purchase Summary

Job Title: Account Coordinator   Price: $195.00
Company: Pacific Ridge Communications   Posting Date: January 5, 2010
Listing Duration: 30 days   Expiration Date: February 4, 2010

Billing Information

First name: [   ]   Last Name: [   ]

Address: [   ]
         [   ]

Country: [Choose... ▼]

City: [   ]   State: [Choose...   ▼]

Postal code: [   ]   Phone: [   ]

Company: [optional]

Figure 11.3 *Enter your billing and credit card information before posting your job.*

Another option for posting jobs on LinkedIn is to post on a relevant group's Jobs Discussion Board. Although there is no cost to post on this board, and you may attract targeted applicants, this type of posting doesn't offer the same level of visibility of a traditional job posting.

Your posted job appears on LinkedIn for 30 days. To manage your open jobs, select Manage Jobs from the Jobs drop-down menu on the global navigation bar. The Manage Jobs page opens, shown in Figure 11.4, where you can

- Complete and post a draft job posting

- View open and closed job postings

- Inform your network about your job postings

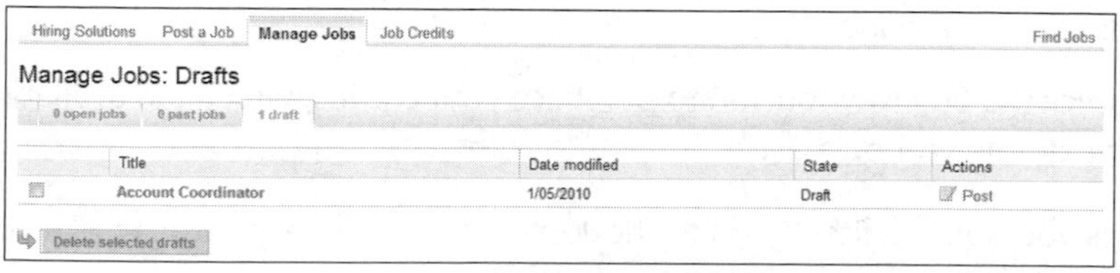

Hiring Solutions	Post a Job	**Manage Jobs**	Job Credits			Find Jobs

Manage Jobs: Drafts

0 open jobs	0 past jobs	1 draft

	Title	Date modified	State	Actions
☐	Account Coordinator	1/05/2010	Draft	✓ Post

Delete selected drafts

Figure 11.4 *Manage drafts, open jobs, and closed (past) jobs on the Manage Jobs page.*

- Search for potential candidates
- Review job applicants' resumes and cover letters
- Perform reference searches

Working with Job Credits

Purchasing job credits can save you money if you post jobs on LinkedIn frequently, yet don't want to upgrade to LinkedIn Talent Advantage. A job credit is a prepaid credit for posting a single job. Job credits come in packages of five or ten credits with discounts off the $195 fee for a single, full-price job posting.

 SHOW ME   Media 11.3—Purchasing LinkedIn Job Credits
Access this video file through your registered Web Edition at
my.safaribooksonline.com/9780789745095/media.

 LET ME TRY IT

Purchasing Job Credits

To purchase job credits, follow these steps:

1. On the global navigation bar, select Post a Job from the Jobs drop-down menu.

2. Click the Job Credits tab to open the Job Credits Summary page.

3. Click the Purchase Credits button. The Purchase: Job Credits page opens, as shown in Figure 11.5.

4. Select the number of job credits you want to purchase: five job credits for $145 per job ($725 total) or ten job credits for $115 per job ($1,150 total).

5. Click the Continue button.

6. Enter your contact and credit card information on the Purchase: Billing Information page.

7. Click the Buy Now button to purchase your credits, which are available the next time you post a job.

To track your job credits, return to the Job Credits Summary page, where you can view details about your active and used credits.

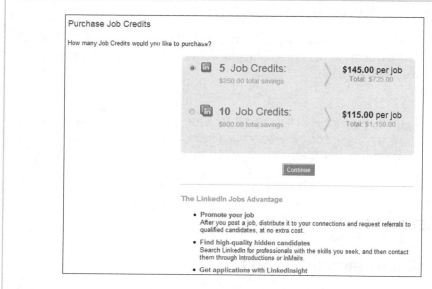

Figure 11.5 *Save money by purchasing LinkedIn job credits.*

Searching for Job Candidates

At times, you may want to search for passive job candidates in addition to considering the candidates who apply directly for your open positions. Here are some search strategies for finding qualified passive candidates:

- Perform an advanced search for LinkedIn members who meet specific criteria. See Chapter 7, "Searching for People on LinkedIn," for more information.

- View the people connecting to your connections who perform a similar function.

- Search LinkedIn Answers for members who provide intelligent answers to questions in your field. See Chapter 14, "Using LinkedIn Answers," for more information.

- Search groups for members whose participation enhances the goals of the group. See Chapter 13, "Participating in LinkedIn Groups," for more information.

If you plan to contact potential job or reference candidates by InMail, consider upgrading to a premium account that includes a specified number of InMails per month. Click the Upgrade Your Account link on the bottom navigation menu for more information.

Performing Reference Searches

LinkedIn reference searches are a premium feature that let you search for LinkedIn members who worked at the same company at the same time as a candidate you're considering for a job.

> If you're a premium member or if you paid for a job posting, you can click the Search for References link on a member's profile or click the Find References link next to a specific applicant on the Manage Jobs page.

 **LET ME TRY IT**

Performing a Reference Search

To perform a reference search, follow these steps:

1. Select the People option on the search box that appears on the global navigation bar.

2. Click the Advanced link to the right of the search box. The Advanced People Search page opens.

3. Click the Reference Search tab, shown in Figure 11.6.

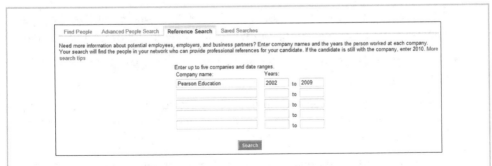

Figure 11.6   *Perform reference searches on potential job candidates.*

4. Enter the company name, optional candidate name, and years of employment in the text boxes. You can search for up to five companies at one time.

5. Click the Search button. The Reference Search Results page displays information about people in your network who meet the criteria you specified.

If you don't have a premium account and haven't posted a job, the returned results will show only the number of people who meet the criteria. To see more details, you need to have a Business or Pro account. Click the Upgrade Now button to view upgrade options.

LinkedIn offers two other ways to search for similar reference information at no cost. You can

- Click the name of a company on a candidate's profile and view the list of current and former employees on the company profile.

- Perform an advanced people search, specifying the candidate's company and location. See Chapter 7 for more information on advanced searches.

Using LinkedIn Talent Advantage

LinkedIn Talent Advantage is LinkedIn's corporate recruiting solution. Major companies (such as Kaiser Permanente, Logitech, Juniper Networks, and Adaptec) use LinkedIn Talent Advantage.

LinkedIn Talent Advantage includes the following components:

- **LinkedIn Recruiter.** Enable a team of recruiters to collaborate, manage the recruitment process, and source passive job candidates. In addition, you receive 50 InMails per month per seat, which you can share across your team.

- **LinkedIn Jobs Network.** Post jobs with precision targeting, candidate match recommendation, and viral distribution.

- **LinkedIn Talent Direct.** Create targeted direct InMail campaigns.

- **LinkedIn Custom Company Profiles.** Enhance company profiles with custom content, including employee spotlights and video.

- **LinkedIn Employer Advertising.** Position your company as an employer of choice through targeted ads.

To learn more about LinkedIn Talent Advantage, click the Recruiting Solutions link on the bottom navigation menu.

12

Enhancing Your Profile with LinkedIn Applications

LinkedIn applications are optional extensions to LinkedIn that enhance the content and effectiveness of your profile, foster collaboration with your network, and integrate your LinkedIn data with other sites to provide further research and competitive intelligence opportunities.

In this chapter, you learn how to add, manage, and remove applications, including events and polls. You can also listen to advice on choosing the right applications for your needs and watch videos that show you how to add applications, create a free LinkedIn poll, add and manage events, and use the WordPress application.

Understanding LinkedIn Applications

The following LinkedIn applications are currently available, with more in development:

- Blog Link by SixApart
- Box.net Files by Box.net
- Company Buzz by LinkedIn
- Events by LinkedIn
- Google Presentation by Google
- Huddle Workspaces by Huddle.net
- My Travel by TripIt
- Polls by LinkedIn
- Reading List by Amazon
- SAP Community Bio by LinkedIn
- SlideShare Presentations by SlideShare
- Tweets by LinkedIn

- WordPress by WordPress

All LinkedIn applications are free, but some require you to have an account with an application that might charge fees based on your usage. For example, Box.net Files and Huddle Workspaces offer both free and fee-based plans.

Choosing the Right Applications

LinkedIn applications offer many options for sharing and collaborating. At times, the number of choices is overwhelming. Although some applications, such as My Travel and Company Buzz, are unique in terms of the features they provide, other applications overlap in their functionality. For example, both Blog Link and WordPress enable you to share blog posts on your profile. You can share presentations using Google Presentation, SlideShare Presentations, and even Box.net Files.

 TELL ME MORE   Media 12.1—Choosing the Right Applications

Access this audio recording through your registered Web Edition at
my.safaribooksonline.com/9780789745095/media.

Here are some tips for making the most of LinkedIn applications:

- Analyze how each application fits into your strategic plan and helps you meet your goals. Just because something sounds interesting doesn't make it worthwhile to add.

- If more than one application performs the same function, compare their features before you pick one to use. Fortunately, LinkedIn applications are easy to add and remove.

- Focus on quality rather than quantity when choosing the documents and presentations you would like to share. A resume, portfolio, or presentation that highlights your business can enhance the effectiveness and reach of your LinkedIn profile, but don't add so many documents that the important ones are lost in the mix.

- Consider your personal privacy with all the documents and data you share online. For example, adding your resume to your profile can aid in your job search, but you might not want to include your home address or phone number.

- Determine whether you have the legal right to post presentations or other documents you created for an employer.

Adding Applications

The basic steps for adding an application are similar for all applications. Once you complete these four steps, you can customize the way you want to use each application.

 SHOW ME   Media 12.2—Adding LinkedIn Applications
Access this video file through your registered Web Edition at
my.safaribooksonline.com/9780789745095/media.

 LET ME TRY IT

Adding an Application

To add an application to your profile or home page, follow these steps:

1. On the global navigation bar, select Application Directory from the More drop-down menu. Alternatively, click the Add Application link on the Edit My Profile page. The Applications page opens (see Figure 12.1).

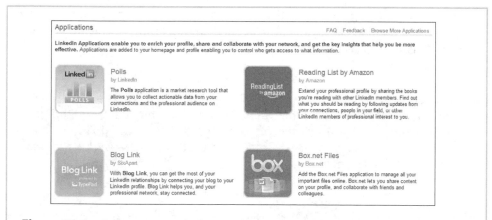

Figure 12.1   *Enhance your LinkedIn experience with one of the many available applications.*

2. Select the application you want to add. The page for that application opens. Figure 12.2 illustrates the Google Presentation page, as an example.

3. The Application Info box appears on the right side of every application page. In this box, choose whether you want to display the application on your profile, on your LinkedIn home page, or on both pages.

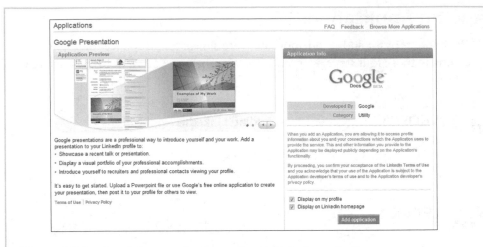

Figure 12.2   *Google Presentation is one of many LinkedIn applications.*

4. Click the Add Application button to add the application and enter details specific to that application.

The rest of this section explains how to set up individual applications.

When you add an application, a link to it appears on the More drop-down menu on the global navigation bar. If you haven't added any applications, only the Reading List by Amazon and Events links appear by default.

You can also add applications from the Edit My Profile page. On the global navigation bar, select Edit Profile from the Profile drop-down menu to open this page. Scroll down to the Applications section and click the Add Application link to open the Applications page. Applications you add will appear in this section if you choose to display them on your profile.

Adding the Blog Link Application

The Blog Link application enables you to post summaries of your blog posts to your LinkedIn profile. You can also follow the blog posts of LinkedIn members in your network. Blog Link supports blogs on multiple platforms including TypePad, Movable Type, Vox, Wordpress.com, Wordpress.org, Tumblr, Blogger, LiveJournal, and more.

WordPress users have two choices for displaying their blog posts on their pro-files: the Blog Link application and the WordPress application. Both applications serve the same function, but they display your blog posts in a different format. If you use WordPress, try both applications to see which one you prefer. See "Adding the WordPress Application" later in this chapter for more information.

Before adding the Blog Link application, verify that the URL to your blog appears in the Websites section on your profile. See Chapter 2, "Creating Your LinkedIn Profile," for more information on listing your blog in this section. The application pulls your blog data from your profile and doesn't work properly if you don't have a blog listed.

To add the Blog Link application, follow the steps listed in "Adding Applications" earlier in this chapter, selecting the Blog Link application on the Applications page. The Blog Link application opens, as shown in Figure 12.3.

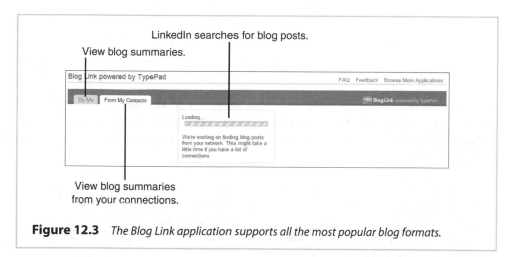

Figure 12.3   *The Blog Link application supports all the most popular blog formats.*

The Blog Link application searches for your blog posts and includes summaries on your LinkedIn profile (see Figure 12.4). They also appear on the From Me tab in the Blog Link application.

If your blog posts don't appear on your profile, verify that you selected the Display on My Profile checkbox on the initial application page. Also, verify that your blog is listed on the Websites section of your profile. The Blog Link application pulls its content from the blog listed in this section.

Figure 12.4 *Automatically post your blog updates to your LinkedIn profile.*

Blog Link also searches for blog posts from your connections and includes these on the From My Contacts tab. If you don't want to view a particular blog, click the Hide This Feed link below its title. Blog posts from other LinkedIn members don't appear on your profile.

Remember that your LinkedIn profile is part of your professional presence online. Include only blog content that supports your professional image. Personal blogs or blogs covering controversial topics might not be suitable to share with your LinkedIn connections.

Adding the Box.net Files Application

The Box.net Files application enables you to share content from Box.net (www.box.net), a leading online collaboration and file-sharing website. With this application, you can post files such as resumes, portfolios, and presentations to your profile, collaborate privately with your LinkedIn connections, and view and edit your files online.

If you don't already have an account on Box.net Files, you can sign up for one from LinkedIn. From here, you can upload files, view your connections' public files, and collaborate privately with your connections.

To add the Box.net Files application, follow the steps listed in the "Adding Applications" section earlier in this chapter, selecting the Box.net Files application on the Applications page.

The Box.net Files application opens, as shown in Figure 12.5.

Figure 12.5   *Use the Box.net Files application to post a resume or portfolio to your profile.*

The files you selected to display publicly on your profile appear in the Applications section, as shown in Figure 12.6.

LinkedIn Profile   Menu | ▼

W Chronological Resume.doc	03/27/09	71 KB
W Functional Resume.doc	03/02/09	53 KB
PDF Value Presentation.pdf	03/27/09	53 KB

Figure 12.6   *Posting a resume can help job seekers stand out from the crowd.*

Adding the Company Buzz Application

Company Buzz is powered by Twitter (www.twitter.com), the popular microsharing site. When Twitter users post tweets (short messages of 140 characters or less) about the companies or schools listed on your profile, you can view them on the Company Buzz page or on your home page.

Company Buzz offers much more than just the latest chatter about your company, however. It's also a great research tool that lets you follow tweets about multiple topics, identify buzz words, and track trends.

To add the Company Buzz application, follow the steps listed in the "Adding Applications" section earlier in this chapter, selecting the Company Buzz application on the Applications page.

The right side of the Company Buzz page displays links to the most recent Twitter tweets about your companies and schools. Each tweet includes a link to its author's Twitter page, its posting time, and links to share, retweet, or reply to a tweet.

The left column of the Company Buzz page contains several boxes that offer additional options. These include the following:

- **Search.** Search Company Buzz by keyword. Click the Save This Search link above the search results to add this search to the Saved Searches box.

- **Saved Searches.** Displays a list of companies, schools, and topics based on the content in your profile. Click each link to view tweets specific to that topic. Click the Manage link to edit or delete a topic.

- **Buzz Words.** Lists the five words most frequently associated with the tweets for your topic. Click a buzz word's link to view only the tweets for that word.

- **Trends.** Displays a chart that shows you the number of tweets related to a topic on a specific day. Figure 12.7 shows a sample trending chart.

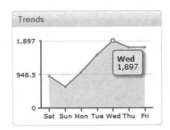

Figure 12.7   *Use Company Buzz to view trends related to the companies, schools, and topics you follow.*

Click the Settings tab to specify whether you want to send a network update to your connections when you save a search in Company Buzz. LinkedIn performs this action by default, but you can remove this check mark if you don't want to let all your connections know about your Company Buzz activity.

Adding the Google Presentation Application

The Google Presentation application lets you share presentations on your profile. You can share a PowerPoint presentation or create a presentation using the free Google Docs application (http://docs.google.com).

To add the Google Presentation application, follow the steps listed in the "Adding Applications" section earlier in this chapter, selecting the Google Presentation application on the Applications page. The Google Presentation application opens, as shown in Figure 12.8.

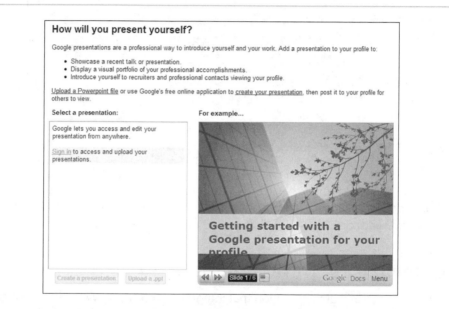

Figure 12.8   *Use Google Presentation to add presentations to your profile to highlight your skills and achievements.*

On this page, you can upload an existing PowerPoint presentation or create a new presentation to share using Google Docs. If you don't already have a Google Docs account, you can sign up on LinkedIn.

Adding the Huddle Workspaces Application

The Huddle Workspaces application enables you to integrate the Huddle online collaboration tool (www.huddle.net) into LinkedIn. With Huddle, you can manage projects online, share files, create and edit documents online, and more. Note that although a basic Huddle account is free, other Huddle plans are fee-based.

To add the Huddle Workspaces application, follow the steps listed in the "Adding Applications" section earlier in this chapter, selecting the Huddle Workspaces application on the Applications page. The Huddle Workspaces application opens, as shown in Figure 12.9.

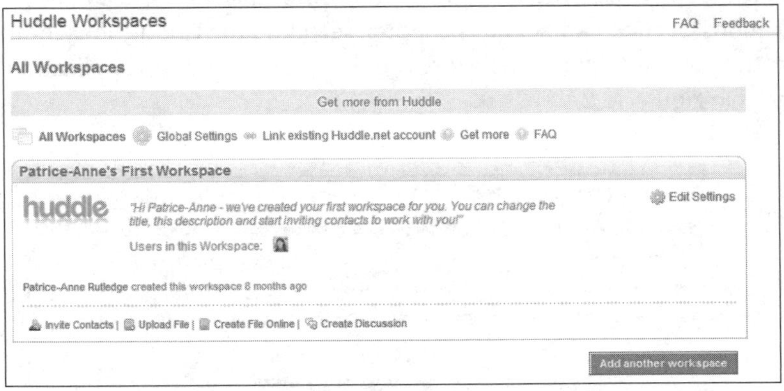

Figure 12.9 *Use Huddle to collaborate online with a private group of LinkedIn connections.*

From here, you can invite your connections to collaborate privately within Huddle's LinkedIn workspace.

Adding the My Travel Application

My Travel is a LinkedIn application that integrates with TripIt (www.tripit.com), the popular travel-planning website. My Travel integrates your TripIt data with your LinkedIn profile and enables you to share travel information with your connections.

LET ME TRY IT

Adding My Travel

To add the My Travel application, follow these steps:

1. Follow the steps listed in the "Adding Applications" section earlier in this chapter, selecting the My Travel application on the Applications page. The My Travel application opens, as shown in Figure 12.10.

2. In the Let's Set Up Your Application box, enter information about your upcoming travel. Although this is optional, it's a good idea to enter any

known travel details. You can also sign up for a TripIt account at the same time, if you don't already have one.

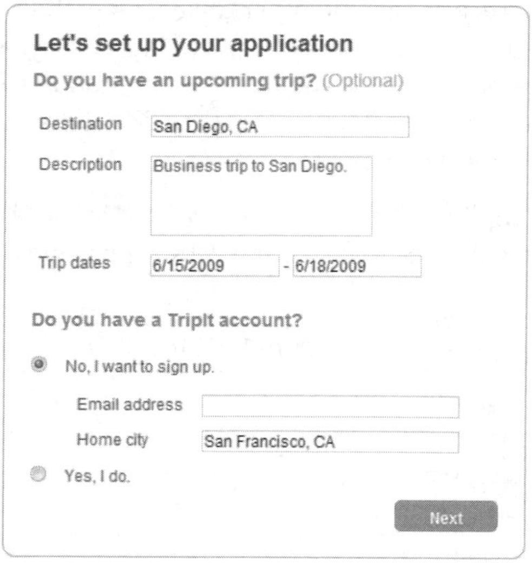

Figure 12.10   *Use My Travel to share your travel plans with your LinkedIn connections.*

3. Click the Next button to open the My Travel page. On this page, you can

   - Click the Summary link to view a summary of your trips, connections who live near your destinations, and your travel stats as compared to your connections.

   - Click the Add Trips link to add more trips.

   - Click the Share Travel Plans link to select up to 10 connections whose travel plans you want to follow. You can add more connections later.

The My Travel application now appears on your profile (see Figure 12.11) and home page (if you selected these display options).

Figure 12.11   *Displaying My Travel on your profile.*

Working with Polls

The Polls application enables you to poll LinkedIn members about relevant professional topics and participate in polls other LinkedIn members create. A LinkedIn poll is a short question with the option of providing as many as five answers. Members select their preferred answer, and the Polls application tallies the results. Polls are different from other applications in that they don't integrate with external data and they offer both free and fee-based options.

To install the Polls application, follow the steps listed in the "Adding Applications" section earlier in this chapter, selecting the Polls application on the Applications page.

The Create a Poll page opens (see Figure 12.12).

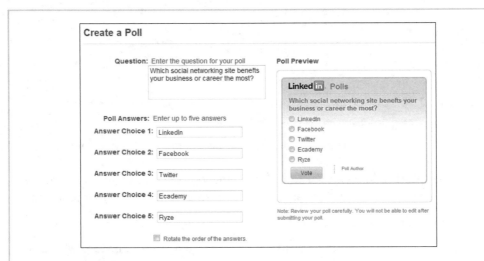

Figure 12.12   *Use a LinkedIn poll to gain valuable insight and perform market research.*

Creating Free LinkedIn Polls

You can invite your 1st-degree connections on LinkedIn to participate in your poll at no charge.

 SHOW ME   **Media 12.3—Creating a Free LinkedIn Poll**
Access this video file through your registered Web Edition at
my.safaribooksonline.com/9780789745095/media.

LET ME TRY IT

Creating a Free LinkedIn Poll

To create a free poll, follow these steps:

1. If the Create a Poll page isn't already open, select Polls from the More drop-down menu on the global navigation bar.

2. Click the Create a Poll tab. The Create a Poll page opens, as shown in Figure 12.12.

3. Enter a question of no more than 125 characters.

4. Enter up to five possible answers to your question.

> Review the Poll Preview box to ensure that your poll is accurate. You can't edit it after submitting, so be careful to avoid spelling, grammar, or content errors.

5. Select the Rotate the Order of the Answers checkbox if you want to vary the position of your answers in your poll.

6. In the Audience section, select the Your 1st-Degree Connections option button. LinkedIn sends a network update informing your connections about your poll. The number of responses you receive will vary based on your number of connections and their interest in participating in your poll. LinkedIn will also provide you with a URL you can use to share your poll with others.

7. Select the Visibility checkbox to include your free poll in the LinkedIn Polls directory, where anyone on LinkedIn can view it and respond. Although there is no guaranteed number of responses, this widens the audience that views your poll.

8. Click the Post Poll button to post your poll to the Network Activity section on your connections' home page.

Creating Paid LinkedIn Polls

If the scope of a free poll doesn't meet your needs, you can purchase a paid poll that surveys a wider audience on LinkedIn. If you choose to purchase a paid poll, you can specify a target audience based on job function, seniority, gender, age, or geography. You pay a set fee (a minimum of $1 per response) with a minimum purchase of 50 responses. If you're a LinkedIn premium member, you might be eligible for discounts or special offers.

LET ME TRY IT

Creating a Paid LinkedIn Poll

To create a paid poll, follow these steps:

1. If the Create a Poll page isn't already open, select Polls from the More drop-down menu on the global navigation bar.

2. Click the Create a Poll tab. The Create a Poll page opens (refer to Figure 12.12).

3. Enter a question of no more than 125 characters.

4. Enter up to five possible answers to your question.

> Review the Poll Preview box to ensure that your poll is accurate. You can't edit it after submitting, so be careful to avoid spelling, grammar, or content errors.

5. Select the Rotate the Order of the Answers checkbox if you want to vary the position of your answers in your poll.

6. In the Audience section, select the Target Audience of Professionals in the U.S. option button.

7. Click the Next Step button to continue to the Plan Your Poll page, as shown in Figure 12.13.

8. To poll all LinkedIn members, select the Show Poll to All LinkedIn Members option button.

9. If you want to narrow your audience, select the Target Specific Members option button and select up to two target categories, such as company size, job function, industry, seniority, gender, age, and geography. Each selected category expands for you to narrow your target audience.

> Targeting specific members adds an additional per response fee to your poll. For example, targeting by company size adds $1.00 per response and targeting by gender adds $0.50.

10. Select the number of responses you want to receive from your poll by dragging the slider below the Enter Number of Responses section. Options range from 50 to 1,000 responses.

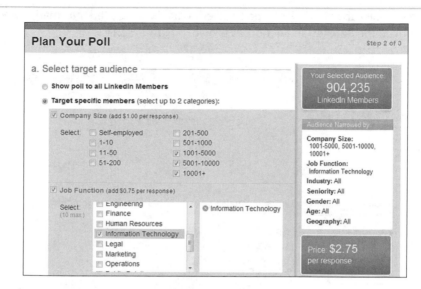

Figure 12.13   *Specify the target audience of your poll.*

11. Click the Next Step button to open the Estimated Runtime for Your Poll pop-up box.

12. LinkedIn displays the estimated runtime for your poll, such as three days. The runtime varies based on how targeted your poll is (the more targeted, the longer the runtime). If you accept this runtime, click the Accept button. If you want to return to the Plan Your Poll page to refine your targets, click the Edit Targets button.

If your poll doesn't receive all the responses you've paid for within the estimated runtime, LinkedIn leaves your poll open until you achieve your target response for a maximum of 45 days.

13. When you accept your runtime, LinkedIn opens the Review Polls & Billing page. On this page, you can preview your poll data, enter your billing details, and agree to LinkedIn's terms and conditions for polls.

14. Click Next Step to post your poll.

Viewing the Results of Your Polls

To view the results of your polls, click the My Polls tab on the Polls page. On this tab, you can select a poll to view, copy a poll to reuse, or end a poll.

When you click the title link of a poll, LinkedIn displays detailed information about your poll in the Poll Results section, as shown in Figure 12.14.

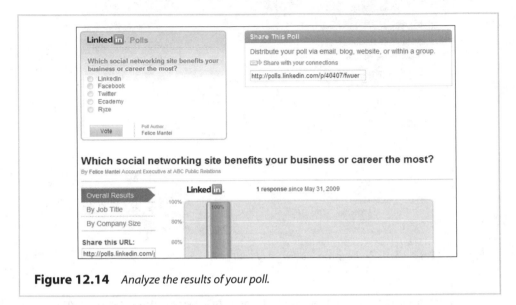

Figure 12.14 *Analyze the results of your poll.*

Here, you can do the following:

- View the total number of responses you've received. Note that each LinkedIn member can vote only once, so no one can skew poll results.

- View the response percentage for each potential answer.

- View responses by job title and company size.

- Share your poll's unique URL with others.

- Add and review comments.

Browsing and Answering Polls

To browse open polls, select Polls from the More drop-down menu on the global navigation bar. The Polls application opens, with the Browse Polls tab selected. On this tab, you can scroll through recently asked polls. To participate in a poll, select the option button for your response and click the Vote button. LinkedIn opens the Poll Results page, where you can view how other LinkedIn members responded to this question.

To view results without voting, click the See Results link below the Vote button.

Adding the Reading List by Amazon Application

The Reading List by Amazon application enables you to share book recommenda-tions and reading plans with your LinkedIn connections. LinkedIn installs the Read-ing List by Amazon application by default.

 LET ME TRY IT

Using the Reading List by Amazon Application

To use the Reading List by Amazon application, follow these steps:

1. On the global navigation bar, select Reading List by Amazon from the More drop-down menu. The Reading List by Amazon application opens, with the Network Updates tab selected. Figure 12.15 shows this tab with updates from your network.

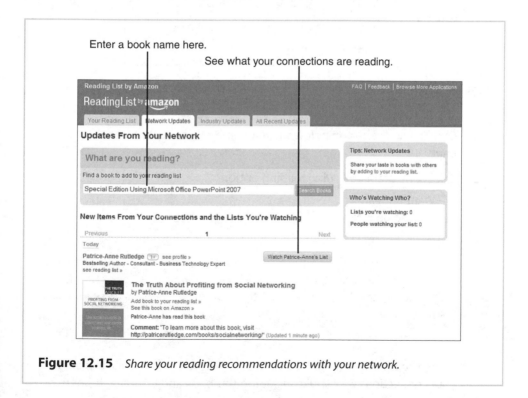

Figure 12.15   *Share your reading recommendations with your network.*

2. In the What Are You Reading section, enter the title of a book you would like to include on your profile.

3. Click the Search Books button to display possible matches (see Figure 12.16). If the book you want to display doesn't appear, revise your search results or search according to author name.

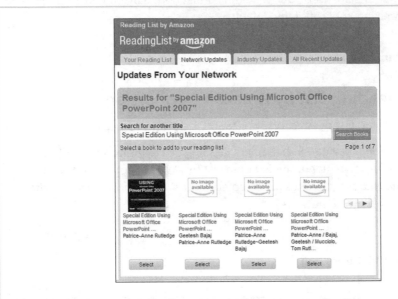

Figure 12.16   *Select the book you want to place on your reading list.*

4. Click the Select button below the matching title to continue to the next page.

5. Select one of the following reading options:
    - I Want to Read It
    - I'm Reading It Now
    - I Read It

If you select the I Read It option button, the I Recommend This Book checkbox appears. Select this checkbox if you want to recommend this book to your connections.

6. Enter a comment of up to 5,000 characters. In your comments, explain to your connections why you're including this book and the value it offers.

7. Select the I'm Reading This Book on My Kindle checkbox if you're reading the Kindle version.

8. Click the Save button to update your reading list.

The book now appears on your profile (see Figure 12.17) and home page (if you selected these display options).

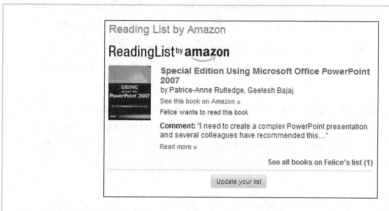

Figure 12.17   *Your connections can view your reading list on your profile.*

To return to this application, select Reading List by Amazon from the More drop-down menu on the global navigation bar. The Network Updates tab is selected by default.

This tab also includes information about the books your connections are reading. For each book that appears, you can click the following:

- Title of the book for more information about the book

- See Profile link to view the profile of the person who recommends this book

- Watch [First Name]'s List button to add yourself to this person's watch list

- Add Book to Your Reading List link to add the book to your own reading list

- See This Book on Amazon link to open the book's Amazon page

In addition to the Network Updates tab, the Reading List by Amazon application also includes three other tabs:

- **Your Reading List.** Displays a list of all books you added to your reading list. You can edit or delete an existing entry from this list.

- **Industry Updates.** Displays books on the reading lists of others in your industry.

- **All Recent Updates.** Displays reading list updates from all LinkedIn members.

Adding the SAP Community Bio Application

The SAP Community Bio application enables members of the SAP Community Network (www.sdn.sap.com) to display membership details on their LinkedIn profiles. This application isn't suited for a general audience; it's for SAP professionals only.

To install this application, follow the steps listed in the "Adding Applications" section earlier in this chapter, selecting the SAP Community Bio application on the Applications page.

On the SAP Community Bio page, click the Login to SCN button to link your SAP Community Network account with LinkedIn. If you choose to display this application on your profile, the SAP Community Bio box lists your name, membership status, and SCN point level.

Adding the SlideShare Presentations Application

Using the SlideShare Presentations application, you can embed presentations and other documents from SlideShare (www.slideshare.net), the popular presentation-sharing site. If you don't have an account on SlideShare, you can sign up for one from LinkedIn and start uploading files. The files you choose appear on your profile.

Although SlideShare is best known for sharing presentations such as PowerPoint files, you can also share videos, webinars, documents, spreadsheets, and PDFs. Files can be up to 100 MB.

To add the SlideShare Presentations application, follow the steps listed in the "Adding Applications" section earlier in this chapter, selecting the SlideShare Presentations application on the Applications page. The SlideShare application opens, as shown in Figure 12.18.

Figure 12.18   *Use SlideShare to incorporate slideshows into your LinkedIn profile.*

If you're new to SlideShare, enter a username, email, and password, and click the Create New Account button.

If you have an existing SlideShare account, click the Here link below the Create New Account button. LinkedIn prompts you to enter your SlideShare username and password and to click the Link to SlideShare button.

The SlideShare application includes the following five tabs:

- **Home.** Displays presentations selected as Editor's Picks for Today as well as presentations from your industry. Click the name of any presentation to view it in a player, tweet it on Twitter, share with your connections, add comments, or mark it as a favorite.

- **Explore.** Displays the most viewed presentations. Also enables you to view presentations with YouTube videos.

- **Your Connections.** Displays presentations your connections have uploaded.

- **Your Slidespace.** Offers the following display options: Your Presentations, Your Favorites, or From Your Industry. You can also click the Your Application Settings link to go to the Settings page. On this page, you can specify whether you want to display presentation thumbnails or complete presentations in a player, as well as modify other network update settings.

- **Upload.** Enables you to upload files to LinkedIn.

Adding the Tweets Application

Using the Tweets application, you can share your latest updates from the popular microsharing site Twitter (www.twitter.com). Options include sharing tweets on your LinkedIn home page or profile.

To add the Tweets application, follow the steps listed in the "Adding Applications" section earlier in this chapter, selecting the Tweets application on the Applications page.

If you haven't already set up LinkedIn to integrate with Twitter, you're prompted to do so before you can access Tweets. See Chapter 2, "Creating Your LinkedIn Profile," for more information about this integration. If don't have a Twitter account, you need to sign up for one on the Twitter website before establishing integration with LinkedIn.

The Tweets application includes three tabs:

- **Overview.** Displays a text box where you can enter a status update on Twitter, a list of people you're following, and the latest tweets from those you follow.

- **My Tweets.** Lists all of your latest tweets.

- **Settings.** Lets you choose whether to display all tweets or only those with the #in or #li hashtag at the end of the tweet. In general, it's best to be selective in the tweets you share. Otherwise, you could share content that's out of context on LinkedIn. Click the Save Settings button to save any changes you make on this page. To go to the Twitter Settings page, click the Go to Settings link.

Depending on your selection when you added the Tweets application, your tweets could appear on your home page, on your profile (see Figure 12.19), or both.

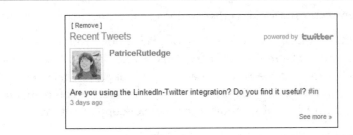

Figure 12.19   *Share your tweets on your LinkedIn profile.*

See Chapter 2, "Creating Your LinkedIn Profile," for information about further LinkedIn and Twitter integration options, such as sharing status updates between the two sites.

Adding the WordPress Application

If you have a WordPress blog, you can display your blog posts on your LinkedIn profile. This application works with both self-hosted WordPress.org blogs and hosted WordPress.com blogs.

If you use a solution other than WordPress to host your blog, check out the Blog Link application instead. WordPress users can choose between adding the WordPress application or adding the Blog Link application. Each application performs the same function, but each displays posts in a different format. See the "Adding the Blog Link Application" section earlier in this chapter for more information.

SHOW ME   Media 12.4—Adding the WordPress Application

Access this video file through your registered Web Edition at
my.safaribooksonline.com/9780789745095/media.

 **LET ME TRY IT**

Adding WordPress

To add the WordPress application, follow these steps:

1. Follow the steps listed in the "Adding Applications" section earlier in this chapter, selecting the WordPress application on the Applications page. The WordPress application opens, as shown in Figure 12.20.

2. Enter the complete URL of your blog in the text box, such as http://www. patricerutledge.com/blog.

3. Indicate whether you want to show all recent blog posts or only those tagged as linkedin.

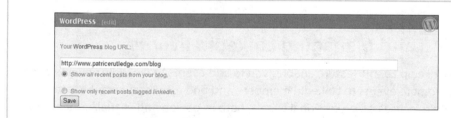

Figure 12.20   *Specify the URL of your WordPress blog.*

Tag your blog posts in WordPress with the "linkedin" tag to select which ones you want to appear on LinkedIn.

4. Click the Save button to preview your blog posts.

Your WordPress blog posts now appear on your profile (see Figure 12.21) and home page (if you selected these display options).

Figure 12.21   *View your blog posts on your LinkedIn profile.*

Adding and Managing LinkedIn Events

The LinkedIn Events feature enables you to add events to LinkedIn's events calendar, promote events to LinkedIn members, and find events you want to attend. LinkedIn focuses on professional events, both in-person and virtual, rather than personal events.

 SHOW ME   Media 12.5—Adding and Managing LinkedIn Events
Access this video file through your registered Web Edition at
my.safaribooksonline.com/9780789745095/media.

LinkedIn installs the Events application by default. To open the LinkedIn Events page, select Events from the More drop-down menu on the global navigation bar. This page contains four tabs:

- **Events Home.** Browse your connections' events, the most popular events on LinkedIn, and event-related network updates. Click an event's title link to view more details, add comments, and RSVP your participation at the event (such as attending, presenting, exhibiting, or interested). This isn't an official RSVP, but rather a way to let your LinkedIn network know about your event activities. You can also see how many other LinkedIn members RSVPed, including your connections.

- **Find Events.** Search for events to attend by keyword, date, location, or event type. Figure 12.22 shows a sample Search Results summary, which also lets you know about your connections' participation.

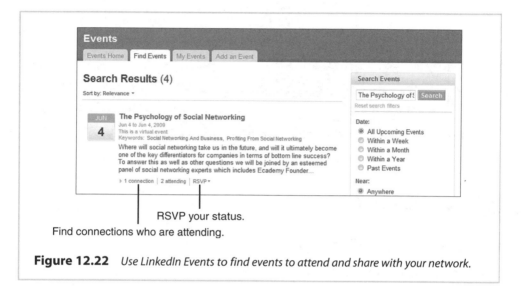

RSVP your status.

Find connections who are attending.

Figure 12.22   *Use LinkedIn Events to find events to attend and share with your network.*

- **My Events.** View a list of the events you added or those events for which you submitted an RSVP.

- **Add an Event.** Add your own events to the LinkedIn events calendar. Figure 12.23 shows a sample new event.

LinkedIn provides event visibility in its event directory, on member home pages, and in member profiles. You can also send a message to your connections about a particular event by clicking the Share link on that event's page. Advertising via LinkedIn DirectAds is another way to promote your event. See Chapter 17, "Advertising on LinkedIn," for more information about placing DirectAds.

Removing Applications

Eventually, you might discover that an application isn't as useful as you thought it would be, and you want to remove it.

Events

Events Home | Find Events | My Events | Add an Event

Add an Event

* Event Title:	Job Search 2.0: Find a Job Faster with Social Networki
* Date & Time:	9/22/2009 5:00pm to 9/22/2009 6:00pm
	☑ This is a virtual event.
Website:	http://www.patricerutledge.com
Are you attending?	○ I'm attending ● I'm interested ○ I'm not attending
Are you organizing?	☑ Yes, I am organizing this event.

⊕ Add more details

[Publish Event] [Preview Event] [Save Draft] or Cancel

* Indicates required fields

Figure 12.23 *Add an event and publicize it on LinkedIn.*

LET ME TRY IT

Removing an Application

To remove an application, follow these steps:

1. On the global navigation bar, select Application Directory from the More drop-down menu.

2. On the Applications page, click the link for the application you want to remove.

3. In the Application Info box on the right side of the page, click the Remove button.

LinkedIn removes the application from your profile and home page.

This chapter shows you how to use LinkedIn Groups to connect with professional peers, potential clients, employers, and partners.

13

Participating in LinkedIn Groups

LinkedIn Groups offer a way for likeminded individuals to share and discuss relevant topics related to the focus of the group. By participating in groups, you can learn from your peers as well as share your own expertise.

In this chapter, you learn how to join and manage groups, participate in group discussions, submit news articles, use a group's jobs discussion board, and create your own groups. You can also listen to tips on maximizing what LinkedIn Groups has to offer and watch videos that show you how to join a group, start a discussion, and post news articles.

Understanding LinkedIn Groups

With LinkedIn Groups, you can

- Research and learn about a wide range of professional topics

- Network and share ideas with industry peers

- Discover job leads and recruit quality talent

- Promote your career or business

 TELL ME MORE   Media 13.1—LinkedIn Groups
Access this audio recording through your registered Web Edition at my.safaribooksonline.com/9780789745095/media.

Remember, to maximize the publicity potential of LinkedIn Groups, focus on visibility and sharing your expertise rather than overt sales or advertising.

LinkedIn Groups take many forms. There are groups for alumni, associations, non-profits, professional interests, corporations, general networking, conference attendees, and personal interests. Your group activity appears on the Group Updates section on your home page, providing additional visibility for your group actions as well as your groups.

LinkedIn imposes a limit of 50 group memberships per account holder. If you reach 50 groups and want to join another, you need to leave an existing group. Because of this limit, it's important to consider carefully which groups will provide you with the most value and help you meet your goals.

Joining Groups

One of the best ways to find a group to join is to search LinkedIn's Groups Directory.

SHOW ME   Media 13.2—Joining LinkedIn Groups
*Access this video file through your registered Web Edition at
my.safaribooksonline.com/9780789745095/media.*

LET ME TRY IT

Joining a Group

To search the directory for potential groups to join, follow these steps:

1. On the global navigation bar, select Groups Directory from the Groups drop-down menu.

   The Featured Groups page opens, shown in Figure 13.1.

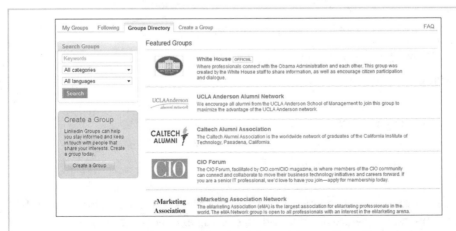

Figure 13.1   *Join a featured group or search for one that meets your criteria.*

2. In the Search Groups box, enter keywords related to the group you want to find. For example, you could enter the name of a company, school, professional association, skill, or hobby.

3. If you want to narrow your search results by category, click All Categories and select a category from the drop-down list. Options include

    - Alumni groups (such as the Cornell University Alumni Group or Club ex-Oracle)

    - Corporate groups (such as HP Connections or Deloitte)

    - Conference groups (such as BIO International Convention or GSMA Mobile World Congress)

    - Networking groups (such as OnStartups or Consultants Network)

    - Non-profit groups (such as Toastmasters International Members or American Red Cross)

    - Professional groups (such as the Medical Devices Group or Project Management Institute Group)

    - Other groups (such as Foodies or the Canon EOS Digital Photography Group)

4. If you want to narrow your search by language, click All Languages and select a language from the drop-down list.

5. Click the Search button to open the Search Results page, which displays a preview of each group that matches your search criteria. The previews boxes include a group description, the group owner's name, and the number of members. Although most groups are open to all LinkedIn members, be sure to clarify this in the group's description. Some groups, for example, require you to be an alumnus of a school or company or a paid member of a professional association. Figure 13.2 shows the Search Results page.

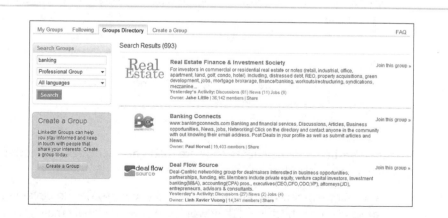

Figure 13.2   *Review the choices that match your keywords on the Search Results page.*

On the Search Results page, you can also click the group title to view more details or click the Share link to share information about this group with your LinkedIn connections.

6. Click the Join This Group link next to the group's description on the Search Results page to open the Join Group page, shown in Figure 13.3.

Join Group

Group Logo:	☑ Display the group logo on my profile.
Contact Email:	Select the email address to use when receiving communications from the group:
	patrice@patricerutledge.com ▼ Add a new email address »
Digest Email:	☑ Send me a digest of all activity in this group.
	Delivery Frequency: Daily digest email ▼
	Note: Your email address will remain hidden from members of this group.
Announcements:	☑ Send me group announcements. (Never more than one a week.)
Messages:	☑ Allow members of this group to send me messages.
	Note: Your email address will remain hidden from members of this group.

Figure 13.3   *Select your group contact preferences on the Join Group page.*

7. If you want the group logo to appear in the Groups section on your profile, select the Group Logo checkbox. Placing this logo on your profile identifies you to fellow members.

8. Specify the Contact Email for sending group announcements and updates.

9. If you want to receive email updates of group activity, select the Digest Email checkbox. You can choose to have updates delivered on a daily basis or a weekly basis.

If you don't want to receive email notifications, you can keep up with your groups on LinkedIn. Your home page displays group updates. In addition, the Updates page for each group summarizes the latest activity.

10. To receive group announcements no more than once per week, select the Announcements checkbox.

11. To allow other members of your group to send you messages on LinkedIn, select the Messages checkbox. (They won't see your personal email address.)

12. Click the Join Group button to join the group.

The My Groups page opens, which lists your current and pending groups. Group managers approve join requests manually unless the group was set up for automatic approval. Your status for a new group on the My Groups page is listed as pending approval. This status remains until the group manager approves you. If you want to follow up with the group owner about a join request, click the Send Message to the Group Manager link. If you want to cancel your request to join the group, click the Withdraw Request link.

Managing Your Groups

LinkedIn offers you lots of flexibility in how you participate in, manage, and view your groups. You can also search for and share specific group information, and leave a group any time you want.

Viewing Your Groups

You can view a list of the groups you belong to by clicking the Groups link on the global navigation bar. The My Groups page opens, shown in Figure 13.4.

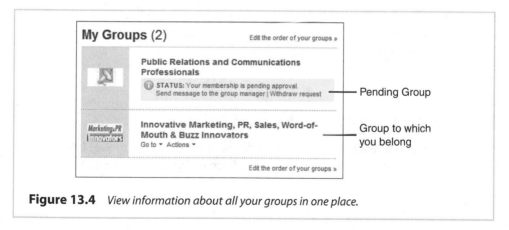

Figure 13.4 *View information about all your groups in one place.*

This page lists all your groups with the following links appearing below each group's name:

- **Go To.** Click the Go To link and select one of the following options from the drop-down list: Overview, Subgroups, Discussions, Jobs, News, Updates, Members, or Settings.

- **Actions.** Click the Actions link and select one of the following actions: Share, Start a Discussion, or Leave Group.

You'll learn more about accessing these group features later in this chapter.

If your request to join a group is still pending, you'll see a notification in that group's preview box. The links to specific tasks aren't available until you're approved for a group. If you are not yet approved, your options include emailing the group manager or withdrawing your request.

If you're the group manager, a Manage link is also available.

You can also view a list of the groups you belong to on your profile.

On the right side of the My Groups page, you'll see summaries of recent group activity from the LinkedIn members you're following. By default, you follow all your connections' activity in groups you both belong to.

To unfollow someone, select Members from the More drop-down menu that appears on the group's detail page. On the members page, you can choose to unfollow the group activity of one of your connections (this doesn't break your connection with this person). Optionally, you can follow the group activity of people who aren't your direct connections by clicking the Follow [First Name] link that appears below their name on the Members tab, as well as several other places within LinkedIn groups.

Managing Group Display Order

For easy access to your groups, LinkedIn displays the first three groups in your My Groups list on the Groups menu you access from the global navigation bar (see Figure 13.5).

Figure 13.5 *Use the Groups menu to access your favorite groups from anywhere within LinkedIn.*

If you're a frequent participant in group activity, it's a good idea to display your favorite groups on this navigation menu. You can also increase the number of displayed groups from three to as many as 10.

 LET ME TRY IT

Changing the Display Order of Your Groups

To change the display order of your groups, follow these steps:

1. On the global navigation bar, click the Groups link.

2. On the My Groups page, click the Edit the Order of Your Groups link. The Groups Order and Display page opens, as shown in Figure 13.6.

Groups Order and Display		
Choose which groups display in what order in the main navigation.		
Groups (36)		
Display the first 3 ▾ groups in the navigation. (Pending groups will not show up)		
Order	**Group Name**	
1	Book Publishing Professionals	Member Settings
2	PRSA Technology	Member Settings
3	ORCL (Oracle) Alumni	Member Settings
4	Club ex-Oracle.org	Member Settings
5	The eLearning Guild	Member Settings
6	Global eLearning Community	Member Settings
7	Consultants Network	Member Settings

Figure 13.6 *Choosing the order in which your groups appear.*

3. Select the number of group links you want to display on the Groups drop-down menu on the global navigation bar. Options range from 1 to 10.

4. Use the Order field to move each of your groups up or down until you reach your desired display order.

You can specify different settings for each of your groups. Click the Member Settings link to make changes to a particular group. See the next section, "Managing Group Settings," for more information.

5. Click the Save Changes button at the bottom of the page to save your changes, which appear on the global navigation bar.

Managing Group Settings

To revise your settings for a group, pause your mouse over the More link on any group page, and then select My Settings from the drop-down list. The Settings page opens, which gives you the option to modify the visibility and contact options for a specific group.

The Settings page is identical to the Join a Group page. See "Joining a Group," earlier in this chapter, for more information on the settings you can modify on this page.

Viewing Group Updates

To view the latest group updates, pause your mouse over the More link on any group page and then select Updates from the drop-down list. The Updates page lists activity for the current and previous day, such as who joined the group, who started a discussion, who posted comments, and so forth. Click the People I'm Following tab to view only updates from the people you follow in this group.

Viewing Group Members

To view a list of group members, pause your mouse over the More link on any group page and then select Members from the drop-down list. This page tells you how many members a group has and displays previews of each group member, starting with you. From there, LinkedIn lists your 1st-degree connections, your 2nd-degree connections, and, finally, all other members.

Each member preview includes

- A photo and link to the member's profile

- Professional headline and location

- The number of connections and recommendations the member has

- Links to follow or unfollow the member's group activity

- Links to send a message and invite to connect (only for members who aren't your 1st-degree connections)

To search a group's member list for members matching specific criteria, enter keywords in the Search Members box and click the Search button. You can also search groups from the quick search box to the right of the global navigation bar. See Chapter 7, "Searching for People on LinkedIn," for more information on searching for people.

Sharing Information About Groups

If you're a member of a particular group that you think your connections would also enjoy, let them know about it by selecting Actions, Share below the group name on the My Groups page. As a reminder, you can click the Groups link on the global navigation bar to open this page.

LinkedIn takes you to your Inbox, where you can send a group link to as many as 50 of your connections. For best results, let your connections know why you recommend this group or why it's appropriate for them.

See Chapter 6, "Communicating with Your LinkedIn Network," for more information about the Inbox and sending messages.

Leaving a Group

If you decide that a group no longer meets your needs or you have to pare down your current group membership to make room for new groups, you can easily leave a group.

To do so, select Action, Leave Group below the group name on the My Groups page. LinkedIn displays a pop-up box asking you to confirm that you want to leave the group. Click the Yes, Leave Group button to remove the group from your My Groups page.

Participating in Group Discussions

Participating in discussions is one of the greatest values of joining a group. With LinkedIn Group Discussions, you can

- View discussion threads for relevant professional information
- Add a comment to a current discussion
- Start your own discussion

As with everything else on LinkedIn, focus on intelligent, meaningful comments that add value to a discussion. Don't post a sales pitch or irrelevant comment just to lead people to your profile.

To view discussions for a group you belong to, click the Groups link on the global navigation menu to open the My Groups page. From here, you have two choices:

- If your group has recent discussion activity, the Discussions link appears below the name of the group. Click this link to access the Discussions tab directly.

- If no Discussions link is available, pause your mouse over the Go To link and click Discussions on the menu that appears.

The Discussions tab displays a preview of the discussions with the most recent activity. Each preview box includes the name and photo of the person who started the discussion, when it was posted, a link to add comments (plus the number of comments), and a link to follow the discussion.

Although Recent Activity is the default view for discussions, you can also click any of the links in the Discussions box on the left side of the page for additional views. Options include

- Recent Discussions

- Most Comments

- My Discussions

- My Comments

- My Followed Discussions

Adding Comments to a Discussion

You can participate in a discussion by adding relevant comments.

 LET ME TRY IT

Adding a Comment to a Discussion

To add a comment to a discussion, follow these steps:

1. Click the Add Comment link in the preview box of any discussion topic that appears on the Discussions tab. If comments already exist, this link displays the number of comments instead. For example, if a discussion already has two comments, you would click the 2 Comments link. The Discussion page opens, displaying the original post as well as the comments of other LinkedIn members.

2. Enter your own comment in the Add a Comment text box, shown in Figure 13.7.

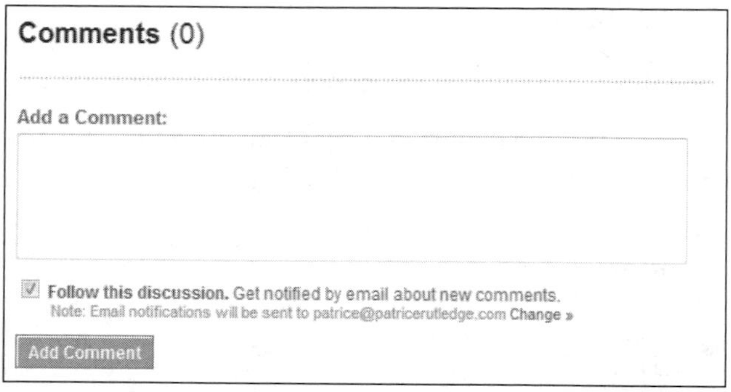

Comments (0)

Add a Comment:

☑ Follow this discussion. Get notified by email about new comments.
Note: Email notifications will be sent to patrice@patricerutledge.com Change »

Add Comment

Figure 13.7 *Contributing your own thoughts to a discussion.*

3. If you want to receive email notification of any new comments in this discussion, select the Follow This Discussion checkbox. You can also view all the group activity you're following by clicking the Following tab on the My Groups page.

4. Click the Add Comment button to post your comment.

To reply privately to the original poster or anyone who posted a comment, click the Reply Privately link.

After you post a comment, LinkedIn gives you 15 minutes to revise it. Click the Edit Comment link below your comment to make any changes. Click the Delete Comment link to remove your comment from the discussion at any time.

Starting Discussions

If you want to start a conversation on a topic that isn't already covered, you can start your own discussion.

 SHOW ME   Media 13.3—Starting a Discussion in a LinkedIn Group
Access this video file through your registered Web Edition at
my.safaribooksonline.com/9780789745095/media.

LET ME TRY IT

Starting a Discussion

To start your own discussion, follow these steps:

1. Click the Start a Discussion link on the Discussions tab. The Start a Discussion page opens, as shown in Figure 13.8.

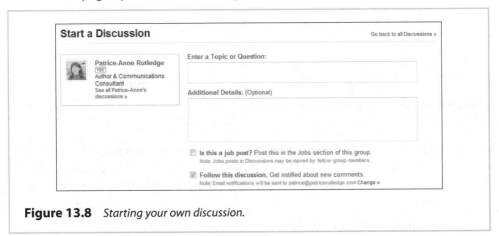

Figure 13.8 *Starting your own discussion.*

2. Enter a topic or question for discussion. To encourage participation, keep the topic or question brief and focused.

3. Enter any optional additional details about your discussion topic. Do you want advice from other professionals? Are you seeking opinions on a newsworthy topic? Be specific about what you seek in member comments.

The Is This a Job Post? checkbox prompts you to consider whether your post is more appropriate for posting under the Jobs tab. See the "Using a Group's Jobs Discussion Board" section later in this chapter for more information.

4. If you want to receive email notification of any new comments in this discussion, select the Follow This Discussion checkbox.

5. Click the Submit for Discussion button to post your discussion topic to the Discussions tab where other members can view and comment on it.

Viewing and Submitting News Articles

Submitting links to news articles and commenting on them is another good way to participate in a group. A news article is a link to an external site such as a newspaper or magazine article or a blog post that's relevant to the topic of the group. For example, you could submit an article you just read in a major newspaper or you could submit a great post from your favorite blog.

Submitting your own articles, blog posts, or media coverage is acceptable, but don't overdo this feature as a promotional tool. Submit only the most informative, meaningful content that offers value to the members of your group.

Viewing News Articles

To view news articles for a group you belong to, click the Groups link on the global navigation bar. On the My Groups page, select Go To, News in the preview box of your target group. The group opens with the News tab selected.

The News tab displays a preview of the news articles with the most activity. Each preview box includes the name of the news source, when it was posted, the number of views, a link to discuss, and the number of discussion comments, if any. You can also pause the mouse over the news article title to open a pop-up box with more details, including a brief summary and the name and photo of the person who submitted the news item.

Although Most Activity is the default view for news, you can access additional views by clicking any of the links in the News box on the left side of the page. Options include the following:

- Latest News

- Recently Submitted

- Recent Discussions

To view the actual news article, click its title link on the News tab. LinkedIn opens the external news item in a shared window.

To exit LinkedIn and move to the external site, click the Close [x] button in the upper-right corner of the screen. To return to the News tab, click your browser's Back button.

Adding Discussion Comments to News Articles

You can add your own comments about news articles, just as you can for discussion topics.

 LET ME TRY IT

Adding a Comment to a News Article

To add a discussion comment to a news article, follow these steps:

1. Click the Discuss link below the news article preview on the News tab. If comments already exist, this link displays the number of comments instead. For example, if an article already has two comments, you would click the 2 Comments link. The News Discussion page opens, displaying the original post as well as the comments of other LinkedIn members.

2. Enter your comment in the Add a Comment text box.

3. If you want to receive email notification of any new comments in this discussion, select the Follow This Discussion checkbox.

4. Click the Add Comment button to post your comment.

After you post a comment, LinkedIn gives you 15 minutes to revise it. Click the Edit Comment link below your comment to make any changes. Click the Delete Comment link to remove your comment from the discussion.

Posting News Articles

You can also contribute to your groups by posting relevant news articles that are of interest to other group members.

 SHOW ME   Media 13.4—Posting News Articles to LinkedIn Groups
Access this video file through your registered Web Edition at
my.safaribooksonline.com/9780789745095/media.

 **LET ME TRY IT**

Posting a News Article

To post a news article, follow these steps:

1. Click the Submit a New Article link on the News tab. The Submit a News Article pop-up box opens.

2. Enter the article URL of the news item you want to post. Be sure to include a complete URL starting with http://.

3. Click the Continue button. Figure 13.9 shows the Submit and Share a News Article page.

Figure 13.9   *Submitting news articles to share with your fellow group members.*

4. LinkedIn suggests a title for this article based on its original source, but you can edit this title if you want.

5. LinkedIn suggests an article summary based on its original source. Again, you can edit this text to better reflect the article's content. LinkedIn displays only the first 250 characters.

6. Enter the news source (such as the name of a newspaper, magazine, or blog).

7. In the Add Comment text box, let group members know why this article is relevant.

8. If you want to receive email notification of any new comments for this news article, select the Follow This Discussion checkbox.

9. Click the Add News Article button to post your article on the News tab where other members can view and comment on it.

Using a Group's Jobs Discussion Board

If you're recruiting for a position that would interest the members of a specific LinkedIn group, you can post your job on the group's Jobs Discussion Board located on the Jobs tab. This is also a great place for jobseekers to find targeted jobs.

For more ways to search for and post jobs on LinkedIn, click the Jobs link on the top navigation menu of the LinkedIn home page. See Chapter 9, "Searching for Jobs," and Chapter 11, "Recruiting Job Candidates," for more information.

Viewing Job Postings

To view job postings for a group you belong to, click the Groups link on the global navigation bar. On the My Groups page, select Go To, Jobs in the preview box of your target group. The group opens with the Jobs tab selected.

The Jobs tab displays a preview of the jobs with the most recent activity. Each preview box includes the name and photo of the person who posted the job, when it was posted, and links to add comments or follow a job's comments.

Although Recent Activity is the default view, you can also click any of the links in the Jobs box on the left side of the page for additional views. Options include

- Recent Jobs
- Most Comments
- My Jobs
- My Comments
- My Followed Jobs

To view the actual job posting, click a job title link.

Adding Comments to Job Postings

If you have questions about a job posting or want to provide input about it to other group members, you can add a comment.

LET ME TRY IT

Adding a Comment to a Job Posting

To add a comment to a job posting you're viewing, follow these steps:

1. Enter your comment in the Add a Comment text box at the bottom of the job detail page.

2. If you want to receive email notification of any new comments related to this job, select the Follow This Job checkbox.

3. Click the Add Comment button to post your comment.

> To reply privately to the original poster or anyone who posted a comment, click the Reply Privately link.

After you post a comment, LinkedIn gives you 15 minutes to revise it. Click the Edit Comment link below your comment to make any changes. Click the Delete Comment link to remove your comment from the discussion.

Posting Jobs on the Jobs Discussion Board

If you have a job that might interest group members, you can create a free job posting.

 **LET ME TRY IT**

Posting a Job to the Jobs Discussion Board

To post a job, follow these steps:

1. On the Jobs tab, click the Post a Job link. The Post a Job page opens, shown in Figure 13.10.

2. Enter a job title that clearly defines the nature of the job.

3. Enter additional details about your job. If you don't want potential candidates to contact you through LinkedIn, be sure to provide different contact information.

4. If you want to receive email notification of any new comments related to the job you post, select the Follow This Job checkbox.

5. Click the Post Job button to post your job to the Jobs tab.

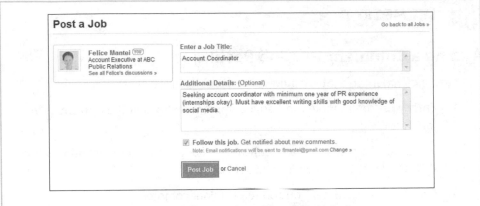

Figure 13.10   *Post a job targeted to members of a specific LinkedIn group.*

Creating and Managing Your Own Groups

In addition to participating in existing groups, LinkedIn enables you to create and manage your own groups. Creating your own LinkedIn group is a great way for the members of a professional, corporate, or alumni association to keep in touch. It can also be a great promotional tool, if managed correctly.

Creating Groups

Creating your own group is a good way to develop a community for a topic, profession, or interest. Before you create a group, consider the following:

- Is there already a similar group on LinkedIn Groups? If so, how will your group differ? What value will you add?

- Is your proposed group an advertisement in disguise? Although many LinkedIn members do benefit from their participation with LinkedIn Groups, you need to create a group whose focus is providing value and community to its members. If you don't, your group most likely won't succeed.

- Do you have the time to maintain and support your group? If you don't respond quickly to join requests and keep the activity going with your group, your group won't flourish.

 **LET ME TRY IT**

Creating Your Own Group

To create a new LinkedIn group, follow these steps:

1. On the global navigation tab, click the Groups link.

2. On the My Groups page, click the Create a Group button. The Create a Group page opens, shown in Figure 13.11.

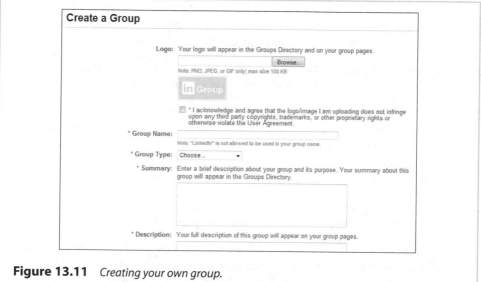

Figure 13.11   *Creating your own group.*

3. Click the Browse button in the Logo section to select and upload a logo for your group. Supported formats include PNG, JPEG, and GIF files no larger than 100 KB.

4. Enter a group name. If your group also exists outside of LinkedIn, you can increase visibility by including the actual group name rather than just an acronym. For example, enter International Association of Business Communicators (IABC) instead of only IABC.

5. Select a group type. Options include alumni, corporate, conference, networking, non-profit, professional, or other groups. The Other group type is most appropriate for special interest or hobby groups that don't fit into any other category.

6. Enter a summary of your group. In this text box, indicate your group's focus, goals, and any membership benefits your group might provide for LinkedIn members. This summary appears in the Groups Directory.

7. In the Description text box, enter more details to display on your group pages.

8. If your group has an external website, enter the URL in the Website field.

9. Enter the group owner email. LinkedIn sends all messages about your group to this email address.

10. If you want to approve group membership requests, select the Request to Join option button. This option is selected by default. LinkedIn sends a message whenever someone requests to join your group, and you must approve the request manually. This requires extra effort on your part, but it ensures that only qualified people join your group. If your group members work for the same organization, you can pre-approve members with a specific email domain by entering it in the text box below.

11. If you want LinkedIn to approve new group members automatically, without your approval, select the Open Access option button.

12. Select the Display This Group in the Groups Directory checkbox or the Allow Group Members to Display the Logo on Their Profiles checkbox if you want to enable these options. These are great promotional tools for your group. Unless you have a specific need for privacy, it's a good idea to make your group visible.

13. Select a language for your group. English is the default language for groups, but LinkedIn offers numerous language choices.

14. If your group is for members who are located in a specific geographic location, select the Location checkbox. The country and postal code field appear so you can specify the exact location of your group.

15. If you agree to the Terms of Service, select the Agreement checkbox. The Terms of Service cover your rights to provide LinkedIn with the email addresses of group members and LinkedIn's rights to use the logo you upload.

16. Click the Create Group button to create your group.

LinkedIn reviews your request to create a new group and approves the group if it meets LinkedIn guidelines.

Managing Your Group

After LinkedIn approves your group, you can start inviting and accepting members.

As a reminder, click the Groups link on the global navigation bar to open the My Groups page where you can access all your LinkedIn groups. To manage your group, select the Manage tab on your group's page.

On the Manage tab, you can

- Approve or reject requests to join your group.

- Send invitations to LinkedIn members, asking them to join your group.

- Upload a pre-approved list of email addresses for your group in CSV format. This option is useful if your group also exists outside of LinkedIn and you know the members you want to pre-approve.

Enter your list of pre-approved members in an Excel file with columns for First Name, Last Name, and Email. Save your spreadsheet as a CSV file. CSV stands for Comma Separated Values, a common text file format.

This chapter shows you how to use LinkedIn
Answers to gain valuable insight from your peers
and demonstrate your own professional expertise.

14

Using LinkedIn Answers

LinkedIn Answers is an interactive feature that enables you to ask questions, receive input from a worldwide network of peers and experts, share your own expertise, and develop your platform as an expert.

In this chapter, you learn how to ask and answer questions, search for specific questions, and rate answers to questions you've asked. You can also listen to advice on profiting from the LinkedIn Answers community and watch videos that show you how to search LinkedIn Answers by keyword, answer a question, and ask a question.

Exploring LinkedIn Answers

Before answering and asking any questions, you should explore LinkedIn Answers to get a feel for the depth of information that's available, the types of questions and answers that people post, and how this platform can help you meet your goals.

Understand that LinkedIn Answers is for genuine information sharing among professional peers. It's not the place for sales pitches (overt or disguised), open requests for help in getting a job, and so forth. That said, asking intelligent, relevant questions and providing useful answers with real value can help meet your job search and business development goals.

 TELL ME MORE   Media 14.1—Using LinkedIn Answers
Access this audio recording through your registered Web Edition at
my.safaribooksonline.com/9780789745095/media.

To view questions and answers, select Answers from the More drop-down menu on the global navigation bar. The Answers page opens, shown in Figure 14.1.

On the Answers Home tab, you can view the following:

- A box with shortcuts for asking and answering questions. LinkedIn recommends five categories based on previous questions you've answered. If you haven't answered questions, this section displays the Answer Now button.

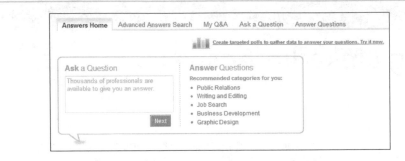

Figure 14.1   *Participate in the LinkedIn community by asking and answering questions.*

- A list of recent questions from your network.

- The week's top experts, based on the number of questions they've answered and the number of times their answers have been selected as best answers.

- The My Q&A box listing your open questions, if any.

- A complete list of LinkedIn Answers categories.

- Links to questions in French, Spanish, German, Italian, and Portuguese, as well as English.

You can ask and answer questions that relate to a variety of professional topics. Categories include the following:

- Administration

- Business Operations

- Business Travel

- Career and Education

- Conferences and Event Planning

- Finance and Accounting

- Financial Markets

- Government and Non-Profit

- Health

- Hiring and Human Resources

- International

- Law and Legal

- Management

- Marketing and Sales

- Non-Profit

- Personal Finance

- Product Management

- Professional Development

- Startups and Small Businesses

- Sustainability

- Technology

- Using LinkedIn

Answering and Managing Questions

LinkedIn Answers contains thousands of open questions at any given time, so it's important to know how to find just the right question, whether you're looking to provide an answer or benefit from the expertise of the LinkedIn members who have already answered. To help you keep up on LinkedIn Answers, you can also subscribe to RSS feeds for your favorite categories.

Finding Open Questions to Answer

The Answers Home tab displays the most recent questions in the New Questions from Your Network section. If you've already participated on LinkedIn Answers, LinkedIn recommends categories based on your past answered questions.

To find more open questions to answer, click the Answer Questions tab. Question summaries appear in the order of their author's connection to you. For example, questions from your 1st-degree connections appear first, and so forth. Click the Date link to sort questions by date instead. In addition to the question title, LinkedIn displays the number of answers the question has received, its author, the date it was posted, and its categories. Figure 14.2 illustrates a sample question summary.

To browse questions relating to a specific category, click one of the links in the Browse box on the right side of the screen. Most categories have subcategories to narrow the subject matter of posted questions even further, as shown in Figure 14.3.

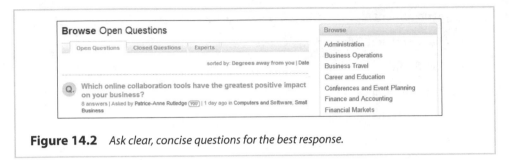

Figure 14.2 *Ask clear, concise questions for the best response.*

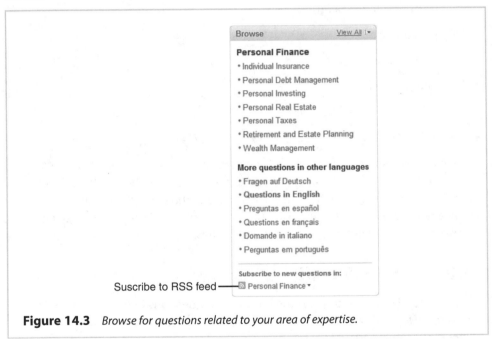

Figure 14.3 *Browse for questions related to your area of expertise.*

You can also browse questions in a specific language. LinkedIn enables members to post questions in English, French, Spanish, German, Italian, and Portuguese.

If you're interested in questions related to a specific category, you can subscribe to the RSS feed for that category. To do so, click the link next to the orange and white feed icon at the bottom of the Browse box. LinkedIn opens the Subscribe Now pop-up box, which enables you to subscribe using your favorite feed reader such as My Yahoo!, Google, or Bloglines. See Chapter 4, "Customizing Your LinkedIn Experience," for more information about subscribing to RSS feeds.

Finally, the Answer Questions tab also offers links for viewing closed questions and popular experts.

If you view a question or answer that you feel is inappropriate, click the Report Question As link or Report Answer As link below it to alert LinkedIn staff. Potential reasons for reporting a question or answer include duplicate posts, open advertising, recruitment messages, inappropriate content, connection-building spam, or misrepresentation.

Searching LinkedIn Answers by Keyword

If you're looking for questions about a specific topic in LinkedIn Answers, performing a keyword search is a good option.

In addition to helping you find specific questions to answer, searching by keyword enables you to

- Discover solutions to your own professional questions from LinkedIn's large collection of information

- Determine what people are asking and saying about you, your company, and your products

- Perform competitive intelligence

 SHOW ME   Media 14.2—Searching LinkedIn Answers by Keyword
Access this video file through your registered Web Edition at
my.safaribooksonline.com/9780789745095/media.

 LET ME TRY IT

Searching by Keyword

To search by keyword, follow these steps:

1. Click the Advanced Answers Search tab on the Answers page. Figure 14.4 illustrates your search possibilities.

2. Enter your search terms in the Keywords field. The more specific your keywords, the more targeted your results will be.

To search on a specific phrase, include that phrase in quotation marks, such as "social media." See Chapter 7, "Searching for People on LinkedIn," for more information about advanced searching techniques.

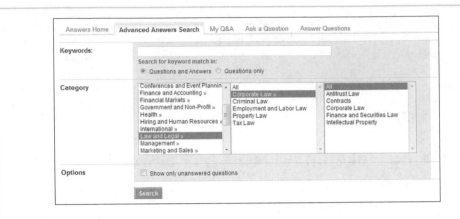

Figure 14.4 *Search LinkedIn Answers for specific keywords.*

3. Specify whether you want to search in Questions and Answers or Questions Only.

4. Select a category and related subcategory in the Category field.

5. If you want to view only questions that haven't been answered, select the Show Only Unanswered Questions checkbox.

6. Click the Search button to display search results.

To view only open questions, click the Open Questions tab. From this page, you can also further refine your search criteria if necessary.

> You can also search LinkedIn Answers from the quick search box on the global navigation bar. Select Answers from the drop-down list, enter your keywords, and click the Search button. Or, click the Advanced link to go directly to the Advanced Answers Search tab.

Answering Questions

Answering questions is a good way to share and demonstrate your expertise in the LinkedIn community. In order to prevent members from "spamming" the Answers forum with too many answers, LinkedIn limits you to 50 answers in 24 hours if you have connections and 5 answers in 24 hours if you don't have any connections yet.

SHOW ME   Media 14.3—Answering Questions on LinkedIn
Access this video file through your registered Web Edition at
my.safaribooksonline.com/9780789745095/media.

LET ME TRY IT

Answering a Question

To post a public reply to a question, follow these steps:

1. Click the Question Title link to view the question's details. Figure 14.5 illustrates a sample question.

2. Click the Answer button to expand the Your Answer box, shown in Figure 14.6.

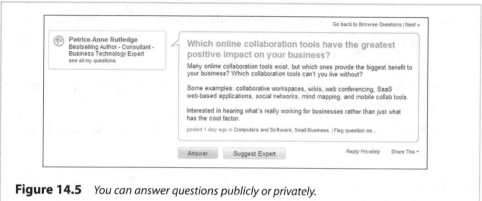

Figure 14.5   *You can answer questions publicly or privately.*

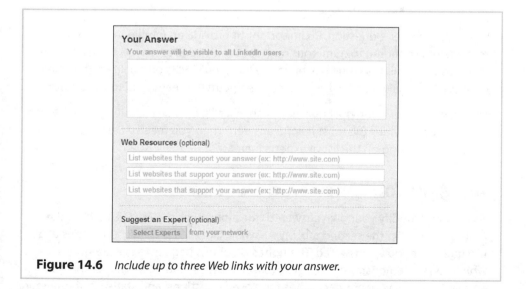

Figure 14.6   *Include up to three Web links with your answer.*

3. Enter your answer in the text box. Remember to provide value and true information. Don't sell your own expertise and services. Let your LinkedIn profile do that for you.

4. Optionally, list up to three Web resources. Include the complete URL, such as http://www.patricerutledge.com.

5. Optionally, click the Select Experts button to open your connection list. You can choose up to three experts from your network to recommend for this question. The experts you suggest appear in your answer with links to their profiles.

6. Enter an optional, private note to the person who posted the question. No other LinkedIn members will see this content.

7. Click Submit to post your answer.

If you don't want to answer a question directly, you can do the following:

- Click the Suggest Expert button to choose expert referrals from your list of connections.

- Click the Reply Privately link to send a private message to the person who posted the question.

- Click the Share This link to email this question to others or post to Delicious.

Sharing LinkedIn questions on social bookmarking sites such as Delicious (www.delicious.com) is a good way to expand visibility.

When you answer a question, it's important to provide an intelligent, helpful response. Responding to numerous questions with vague answers in an effort to increase your visibility won't pay off in the long run. Focus on quality rather than quantity, and answer only when you have something meaningful to contribute.

LinkedIn members who post questions can award a best answer designation to the person who provides the most helpful answer. When you receive Best Answer votes, your ranking on the list of experts increases.

Managing Your Answered Questions

To view and modify your own answered questions, click the My Q&A tab on the Answers page. On the second tab, My Answers, LinkedIn displays summaries of all the questions you've answered. The right side of this page lists the categories in which you've demonstrated expertise (based on receiving "best answer" or "good answer" ratings), your answer ratings for closed questions, and statistics about your activity on LinkedIn Answers. Figure 14.7 shows a sample member's expertise rating.

You can modify or delete your answers to open questions only. Click the Clarify My Answer link to add clarification to your existing answer. Click the Delete My Answer link to delete your answer.

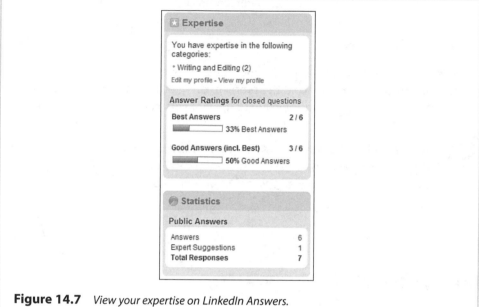

Figure 14.7   *View your expertise on LinkedIn Answers.*

Your activity on LinkedIn Answers also appears in the Q&A box on the right column of your profile, shown in Figure 14.8.

This box lists your questions, answers, and expertise. If you've received any best answer votes, a green square with a white star appears in this box. To remove the Q&A box from your profile, click the Change This Setting link.

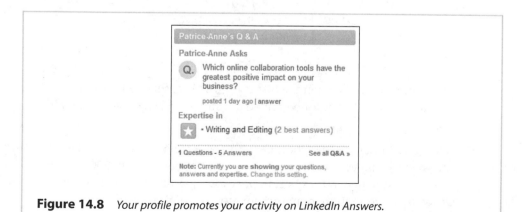

Figure 14.8   *Your profile promotes your activity on LinkedIn Answers.*

Asking and Managing Questions

In addition to answering questions and searching existing questions for useful information, you can also ask the LinkedIn community your own questions.

Asking Questions

LinkedIn members can ask up to ten questions a month on LinkedIn Answers. LinkedIn imposes a limit to avoid the problem of "question spam" and to focus members on asking questions of value to the LinkedIn community.

 SHOW ME   Media 14.4—Asking Questions on LinkedIn Answers
Access this video file through your registered Web Edition at
my.safaribooksonline.com/9780789745095/media.

 LET ME TRY IT

Asking a Question

To ask a question, follow these steps:

1. Select Answers from the More drop-down menu on the global navigation bar.

2. Click the Ask a Question tab to open the Ask a Question page. Figure 14.9 illustrates the Ask a Question page.

> You can also ask your question in the Ask a Question box on the LinkedIn Answers Home tab. When you click Next, LinkedIn takes you to the Ask a Question tab, where you can complete your question.

3. Enter a one-line question in the first text box. Make sure your question is clear and concise. Vague, open-ended questions rarely receive good feedback.

4. Select the Only Share This Question with Connections I Select checkbox if you want to send your question only to specific people (up to 200 of your connections). In general, it's best to post your question to the public LinkedIn Answers forum for maximum response and visibility.

Figure 14.9   *Ask a question and get answers from LinkedIn's millions of members.*

5. Provide pertinent background information in the Add Details box to clarify your question further. Be careful, however, of adding too much detail. Many people skip over very lengthy questions.

6. Categorize your question based on the available categories and subcategories. You can add a second category if desired.

7. If your question is location-specific, select the My Question Is Focused Around a Specific Geographic Location checkbox. LinkedIn prompts you to select a country and optional postal code.

8. Specify whether your question relates to one of the following:
   - Recruiting
   - Promoting Your Services
   - Job Seeking

> If your question relates to recruiting, promotion, or a job search, LinkedIn offers links to other features that might be more appropriate than LinkedIn Answers.

9. Click the Ask Question button to post your question.

LinkedIn's millions of members now have the opportunity to view and answer your question, providing valuable feedback and information.

LinkedIn automatically closes your question in seven days, but offers you the choice to extend the question another week or close it manually before seven days. See the next section, "Managing Your Questions," for more information.

One final step is to rate the answers to your questions based on the value they provide. See "Rating Answers to Your Questions" later in this chapter.

Managing Your Questions

To view and modify your questions, click the My Q&A tab on the Answers page. On the first tab, My Questions, LinkedIn displays a summary of the questions you've asked. Click the link of any question to view it, and if it is still open, make changes. Figure 14.10 illustrates a sample open question.

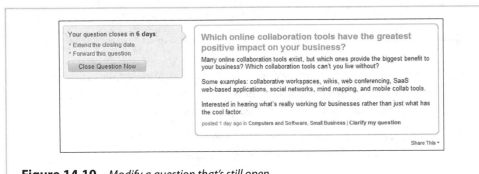

Figure 14.10   *Modify a question that's still open.*

If the question is still open, you can do the following:

- Click the Extend the Closing Date link to extend the closing date by seven days.

- Click the Forward This Question link to send the question to up to 200 of your connections.

- Click the Close Question Now button to close the question before it closes automatically in seven days. You also have the option of hiding your closed question from public view. In general, it's best to keep your question open and allow it to remain on LinkedIn Answers for maximum visibility. If you make a mistake or no longer want to display your question, however, you can close and hide it.

- Click the Clarify My Question link, below the question itself, to open the Clarify Your Question page, where you can add related details. LinkedIn doesn't allow you to edit the question you posted.

Rating Answers to Your Questions

If your question is closed, you can rate the answers you received. Rating answers provides feedback to the LinkedIn Answers community and rewards those who respond with meaningful advice.

 LET ME TRY IT

Rating an Answer to a Question

To rate answers, follow these steps:

1. On the My Questions tab, click the Rate Answers link next to the question whose answers you want to rate (see Figure 14.11).

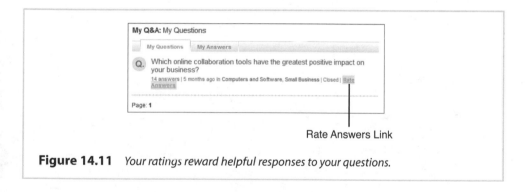

Figure 14.11 *Your ratings reward helpful responses to your questions.*

2. On the Select Good Answers page, select the checkbox next to the most beneficial answers. If you select only one answer, LinkedIn rates it as the best answer. If you select multiple answers, LinkedIn rates them as good answers.

3. Click the Rate button to complete your ratings.

This chapter shows you how to make the most of the LinkedIn Service Providers feature, whether you're seeking to hire service providers or provide services yourself.

15

Using LinkedIn Service Providers

LinkedIn Service Providers connects members searching for service providers with members who provide services. If you're searching for a service provider, you can review peer recommendations before hiring. If you provide professional services, you can receive client recommendations and promote your services to prospective buyers through the LinkedIn database of service providers.

In this chapter, you learn how to find qualified professionals in the LinkedIn Service Providers directory, recommend service providers, and request recommendations. You can also listen to tips about the best ways to use this feature and watch videos that show you how to search for service providers, recommend service providers, and request service provider recommendations.

Understanding Service Providers

The LinkedIn Service Providers directory provides valuable insight for anyone searching for a quality professional to hire for a variety of services. It's also a great tool for consultants and small business owners seeking clients and publicity. It's important, however, to understand just what types of services are a good match for this directory.

LinkedIn offers numerous categories and subcategories of service providers. These include

- Art, Creative and Media: Graphic/Web Designer, Photographer, and Writer/Editor
- Consulting: Business Consultant and IT Consultant
- Employment Services: Career Coach and Recruiter
- Financial & Legal Services: Accountant, Attorney, Financial Advisor, Insurance Agent, and Real Estate Agent
- Health & Medical: Dentist, Doctor, and Personal Trainer

- Home & Garden: Architect, Gardener, General Contractor, Handyman, and House Cleaner

- Other Professional Services: Child Care Provider, Travel Agent, and Veterinarian

If what you're searching for—or what you have to offer—fits into one of these categories, then it's worthwhile for you to explore LinkedIn Service Providers.

TELL ME MORE   Media 15.1—LinkedIn Service Providers

Access this audio recording through your registered Web Edition at
my.safaribooksonline.com/9780789745095/media.

If you're not a service provider, ask for a colleague or business partner recommendation rather than a service provider recommendation. See Chapter 10, "Managing LinkedIn Recommendations," for more information.

Searching for Service Providers

Finding the right service provider is a straightforward process. On the global navigation bar, select Companies from the More drop-down menu. Then click the Service Providers link on the right side of the Companies page.

Figure 15.1 illustrates the Service Provider Recommendations page.

Figure 15.1   *Learn about the service providers your fellow LinkedIn members recommend.*

SHOW ME   Media 15.2—Searching for Service Providers

Access this video file through your registered Web Edition at
my.safaribooksonline.com/9780789745095/media.

By default, LinkedIn lists summaries of the most recent recommendations from all members, but you can click the buttons at the top of the page to modify what appears. Options include displaying only your own recommendations, displaying recommendations from 1st-degree connections, or displaying recommendations from your 2nd-degree network.

Recommendation summaries include the following information (see Figure 15.2):

- The name of the provider with a link to more detailed recommendation information

- A box to the left of the provider's name with the number of recommendations that person has received

- The category and location of the provider

Figure 15.2   *LinkedIn lets you know how many recommendations a provider has received.*

Although the LinkedIn Service Providers directory can help you find quality professionals to perform specialized tasks, it's important to analyze recommendations before making a hiring decision. Who are the people making the recommendations? Do the recommendations include valid insight into the provider's performance or are they vague compliments? How many recommendations does a particular provider have? In many cases, the quantity of recommendations is less important than the quality of the recommendations.

To search for a specific type of service provider, click the appropriate service category in the Categories box on the right side of the page. LinkedIn narrows the results on the Service Providers page to providers only in that category.

If you want to find providers who live in your local area, click the Change Location link. Select a country and optional postal code, and then click the Change Location button to view providers in that geographic area. Alternatively, you can choose one of the top locations for service providers.

Recommending Service Providers

If a LinkedIn member provides outstanding service, you can write this person a service provider recommendation.

 SHOW ME   Media 15.3—Recommending a Service Provider on LinkedIn
Access this video file through your registered Web Edition at my.safaribooksonline.com/9780789745095/media.

 LET ME TRY IT

Recommending a Service Provider

To recommend a service provider, follow these steps:

1. On the global navigation bar, select Companies from the More drop-down menu.

2. On the Companies page, click the Service Providers link.

3. Click the Make a Recommendation tab.

4. Click the Select from Your Connection List link to open your connection list in another window.

5. Select the person you want to recommend. LinkedIn returns to the Make a Recommendation tab.

If you're not connected to the person you want to recommend, enter that person's name and email address. You can even recommend a provider who isn't a LinkedIn member.

6. Click the Continue button.

7. Select the position for which you're recommending the person from the drop-down list (see Figure 15.3). This should be the position associated with the service provider's business.

8. Select a service category from the drop-down list.

9. In the Year First Hired field, indicate when you first start working with this service provider.

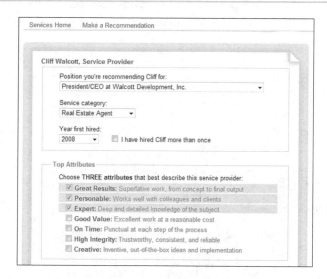

Figure 15.3 *Recommend top service providers so others can find them in LinkedIn's Service Provider directory.*

10. If you've worked with this person before, select the I Have Hired [First Name] More than Once checkbox.

11. Select up to three attributes for this service provider. LinkedIn enables you to choose only three, so consider carefully which are the most applicable. Options include the following:

    - Great Results
    - Personable
    - Expert
    - Good Value
    - On Time
    - High Integrity
    - Creative

12. Enter your recommendation in the Written Recommendation text box. Provide specific, concise reasons why you're recommending this person. Vague accolades or short comments like "great guy" don't make effective recommendations. Instead, focus on actual accomplishments and quantifiable achievements. For example, "Jeff sold our house in 15 days for over the asking price" or "Maura's online marketing campaign increased our website traffic by 30 percent."

13. Click the Send button to send a notification message to the provider that you recommend.

In this message, shown in Figure 15.4, the provider can accept the recommendation, request a replacement recommendation, or archive the recommendation for future consideration.

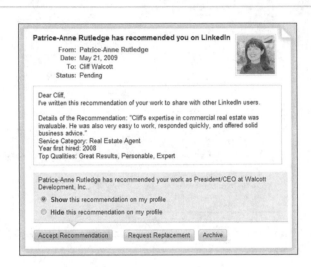

Figure 15.4 *Providers have the option of accepting or asking for changes on any recommendation they receive.*

Providers also have the choice to display or hide your recommendation on their profile. Figure 15.5 shows a provider profile recommendation.

Figure 15.5 *Providers can display recommendations for their connections—and potential clients—to see.*

You can edit or withdraw (delete) a service provider recommendation just as you can any other recommendation. On the global navigation bar, select Recommendations from the Profile drop-down menu and then select the Sent Recommendations tab to make your changes. See Chapter 10, "Managing LinkedIn Recommendations," for more information.

Requesting Service Provider Recommendations

If you're a service provider, you don't need to wait for a client to submit a recommendation for you. You can send a request on LinkedIn asking for a recommendation.

 SHOW ME   Media 15.4—Requesting a LinkedIn Service Provider Recommendation
Access this video file through your registered Web Edition at ***my.safaribooksonline.com/9780789745095/media.***

 LET ME TRY IT

Requesting a Service Provider Recommendation

To request a service provider recommendation, follow these steps:

1. On the global navigation bar, select Companies from the More drop-down list.

2. On the Companies page, click the Service Providers link.

3. On the Service Providers page, click the Request a Recommendation link. Figure 15.6 shows the Request Recommendations page.

4. In Step 1, choose the position for which you want the recommendation from the drop-down list. This should be the job associated with your work as a service provider.

5. In Step 2, select connections to ask for a recommendation. Click the View All Connections icon to select from a list of your connections. Although you can contact up to 200 connections, it's a much better practice to contact one person at a time and customize your request.

6. When you're finished selecting connections, click the Finished button to return to the Request Recommendations page.

7. In Step 3, you can use the sample text LinkedIn provides or, preferably, replace it with a personalized message.

8. Click the Send button to send your recommendation request for completion and approval.

Read the next section, "Responding to a Service Provider Recommendation Request," to learn more about what happens after you send your request.

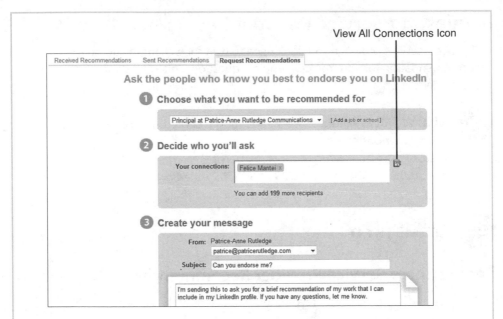

Figure 15.6 *Request a recommendation to gain visibility in the Service Providers directory.*

Because a recommender can provide three types of recommendations, be sure to ask for a service provider recommendation.

Responding to Service Provider Recommendation Requests

When someone requests a service provider recommendation from you, LinkedIn sends a message with "Can You Endorse Me?" as the default subject line.

 **LET ME TRY IT**

Responding to a Service Provider Recommendation Request

If you want to respond to a service provider recommendation request, follow these steps:

1. Click the subject line to open the recommendation request.

2. Click the Write Recommendation button to open the Select Type page.

3. Select Service Provider as the recommendation type you want to write.

4. Click the Continue button to open the Create Your Recommendation page. The fields on this page are the same whether you take the initiative to create a service provider recommendation or respond to a request for one. See "Recommending a Service Provider," earlier in this chapter, for details about how to complete this page.

This chapter shows you how to search for companies that meet your target criteria and add a profile for your own company.

16

Creating a Company Profile

LinkedIn's Company Profiles feature provides an opportunity for companies to present their products, services, and job openings to LinkedIn's vast audience. In addition, company profiles offer extensive data that's particularly useful to job seekers, recruiters, and members searching for potential clients and partners.

In this chapter, you learn how to search company profiles by company name and keyword as well as how to create, manage, and edit your own company profile. You can also listen to advice on making the most of the Company Profiles feature and watch videos that show you how to search company profiles by keyword and add a company profile.

Understanding LinkedIn Company Profiles

Company profiles aren't just for large corporations. If you own a small business, even a one-person business, creating a company profile can help you gain visibility on LinkedIn.

 TELL ME MORE   Media 16.1—LinkedIn Company Profiles

Access this audio recording through your registered Web Edition at my.safaribooksonline.com/9780789745095/media.

Remember, however, that a company profile isn't an advertisement in disguise. Stick to the facts and avoid hype. Read other profiles in your industry before creating your own to understand what is and isn't appropriate.

Figure 16.1 shows a sample company profile.

Company profiles can include the following:

- A company summary

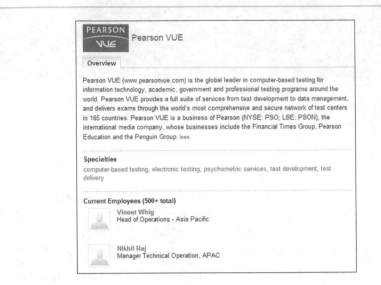

Figure 16.1 *Learn more about a particular company through its profile.*

- A list of specialties with keyword links
- A follow link that enables you to follow a company's activity on LinkedIn
- A list of current employees, including those in your network
- Former employees in your network
- New hires
- Recent promotions and changes
- A list of employees with the most profile views
- Data about related companies
- Key statistics including top locations, company size, website link, common job titles, and median age of employees
- Links to open jobs posted on LinkedIn, if any
- Links to company news
- Stock information

Consider creating a custom company profile, a paid feature that's part of LinkedIn Talent Advantage (http://talent.linkedin.com/profiles). Custom profiles can include additional features such as polls, videos, employee spotlights, and dynamic content that adapts to viewer profiles.

The company profile icon to the right of any company name in a member profile indicates that the company has a listing in LinkedIn Company Profiles. Click the company link to view the complete profile or hover over it to view a preview. Figure 16.2 shows a sample preview.

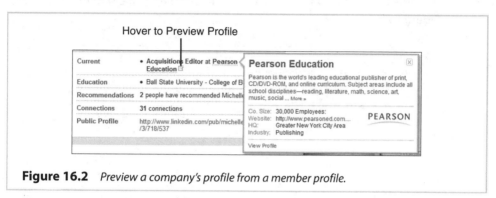

Figure 16.2   *Preview a company's profile from a member profile.*

If a company doesn't have a link or a company profile icon, no company profile exists yet.

Searching Company Profiles

There are two main ways to search company profiles on LinkedIn—by company name and by keyword.

Searching Company Profiles by Company Name

If you know the name of the company you want to find, you can search for it directly.

LET ME TRY IT

Searching by Company Name

To search for a company by name, follow these steps:

1. On the global navigation bar, select the Companies option in the quick search box.

2. Enter the company name in the text box.

3. Click the Search button. The Search Results page appears, shown in Figure 16.3.

Figure 16.3 *Select a profile to view from the search results.*

4. On the Company Search Results page, click the name of the company whose profile you want to view.

If your initial search didn't locate the profile you want to view, edit your criteria in the Modify Your Search box. This box duplicates the fields found on the Search Companies page, described later in this chapter. It's also possible that a profile doesn't exist yet for the company you're searching for.

Searching Company Profiles by Keyword

A quick search works well if you know the company profile you want to view. At times, however, you might want to search Company Profiles to find companies that fit target criteria rather than locate a company you already know.

SHOW ME   Media 16.2—Searching for Company Profiles by Keyword
Access this video file through your registered Web Edition at
my.safaribooksonline.com/9780789745095/media.

 LET ME TRY IT

Searching by Keyword

To search for companies based on criteria you specify, follow these steps:

1. On the global navigation bar, select Companies from the More drop-down menu. The Companies page opens, shown in Figure 16.4.

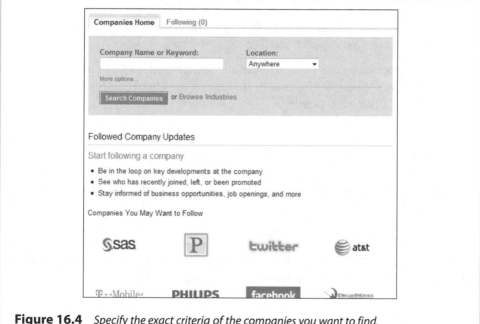

Figure 16.4   *Specify the exact criteria of the companies you want to find.*

2. In the Company Name or Keyword field, enter keywords targeted to your search. For example, enter "investor relations" to search for companies offering this service. You can also enter a company name, but using the quick search box is a faster way to locate a company whose name you already know.

3. By default, LinkedIn searches for companies anywhere in the world. If you want to narrow search results to a specific location, select Located in or

Near from the Location drop-down list and enter a country and optional postal code.

4. To display company headquarter locations only, select the Only Company Headquarters checkbox. This option appears only if you narrow search results by location.

5. Click the More Options link to expand your options.

6. Select an industry from the drop-down list.

7. Search All Companies or limit your search to only companies where you have 1st- or 2nd-degree connections.

8. Specify a target company size from the eight options.

9. If you want to view only companies with current openings, select the Only Companies with Jobs Posted on LinkedIn checkbox.

10. Click the Search Companies button. The Company Search Results page opens with a list of potential matches.

11. Click a company link to view its profile. See "Understanding LinkedIn Company Profiles," earlier in this chapter, to learn more about the information available on a company profile.

You don't need to complete all the fields on the Companies page to perform a search. In fact, you'll generate the best results by starting with your most important criteria and then modifying your criteria only if your initial search doesn't yield the desired results.

In addition to entering search criteria, you can also browse companies by industry by clicking the Browse Industries link on the Companies page.

Adding Company Profiles

If your company isn't listed in Company Profiles, you can create a profile for it. Creating a company profile is a particularly good option for small businesses or solopreneurs seeking to promote their business on LinkedIn.

 SHOW ME   Media 16.3—Adding a Company Profile in LinkedIn
Access this video file through your registered Web Edition at
my.safaribooksonline.com/9780789745095/media.

 **LET ME TRY IT**

Adding a Company Profile

To add a profile for your company, follow these steps:

1. On the global navigation bar, select Companies from the More drop-down menu.

2. Click the Add a Company link at the top of the Companies page. The Add a Company page opens, shown in Figure 16.5.

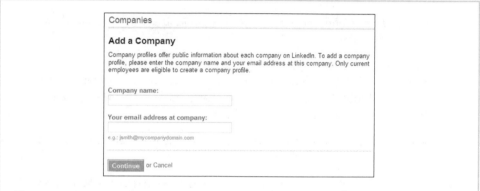

Figure 16.5 *Create a profile for your company for added visibility.*

3. Enter your company name and your email address at company.

4. Click the Continue button. The Companies page opens (see Figure 16.6), prompting you to add basic information for your company.

5. Your Company Name and Email Domain(s) appear by default. Click the Edit link to change these, if desired.

6. Enter your company's website URL.

7. Enter a description of your company. Think strategically about how you want to present your company in this field, focusing on who you want to attract and what action you want them to take. Remember, though, that your description should be factual. This isn't the place to advertise or promote.

8. Select an industry from the drop-down list.

9. Enter the number of employees.

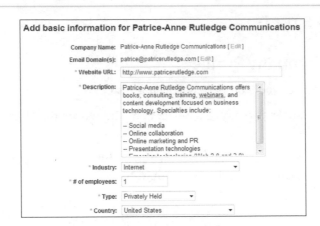

Figure 16.6 *Enter information about your company, including a detailed description.*

10. Select a type for your business. Options include Public Company, Privately Held, Non-Profit, Government Agency, Partnership, Sole Proprietorship, Self-Employed, or Educational Institution.

11. Select your country from the drop-down list and enter an optional postal code.

12. Select your position from the drop-down list. Alternatively, enter a new position.

13. Click the Save & Continue button. The Company Logo page opens.

14. Browse to select a logo. Your logo should be approximately 100 X 60 pixels; in PNG, JPEG, or GIF format; and no more than 100 KB in size.

15. Click the Upload Logo button to upload your logo.

16. Click the Locations link to edit headquarters information or add another location.

17. Click the Financial link to add revenue information.

18. Click the Company Blog link to add the URL of your company blog. LinkedIn displays this data in the News box on your profile.

19. Click the Save Changes button to save changes.

20. Click the Back to Company Profile link to view your profile.

The My Company Profile box, shown in Figure 16.7, now displays on the right side of the Companies page.

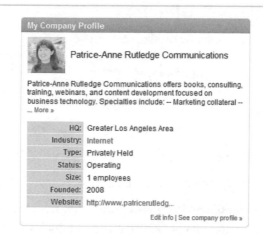

Figure 16.7 *Summary information about your company displays on the Companies page.*

Associating Employees with a Company Profile

LinkedIn associates employees automatically with the company profiles of the current employers that they list on their profiles. If LinkedIn doesn't list you correctly as an employee of your company, you can edit your company information.

 LET ME TRY IT

Associating Employees with Your Company Profile

To associate employees with a company profile, follow these steps:

1. On the global navigation bar, select Edit Profile from the Profile dropdown menu. The Edit My Profile page opens.

2. Click the Edit link next to your current position. The Edit Position page opens.

3. Click the Change Company link and enter a new company name. When you start typing, LinkedIn suggests possible matches. Be careful to choose the correct match. With larger companies in particular, you might find subsidiaries, divisions, or even incorrect spellings.

4. Click the Update button to update your profile.

If LinkedIn members incorrectly identify themselves as employees of your company, contact LinkedIn's Customer Service to have them removed.

Editing Company Profiles

If you added your own company profile, you can edit it if you log in using the same account used to create your profile. You can edit a company profile that you didn't create only if you are a current employee.

 LET ME TRY IT

Editing Your Company Profile

To edit a company profile, follow these steps:

1. On the global navigation bar, select Companies from the More drop-down menu. The Companies page opens, displaying the My Company Profile box in the upper-right corner (refer to Figure 16.7).

2. Click the Edit Info link in the My Company Profile box. Remember, if you didn't create this company profile, LinkedIn prompts you to enter a current company email address before letting you continue.

3. Enter your changes on the Basic Information page.

4. Click the links in the Company Profile box to make changes to your logo, location, financial information, company blog, or related company data.

5. Click the Save Changes button to update your company profile.

See the "Adding a Company Profile" section earlier in this chapter for more information about the data you can enter on a company profile.

This chapter introduces you to LinkedIn advertising options, including DirectAds.

17

Advertising on LinkedIn

LinkedIn offers two advertising programs that focus on reaching the site's highly targeted demographics with ads placed on the home page and member profiles. The LinkedIn audience is comprised of LinkedIn's millions of members around the world with an average household income of $109,000 per year. LinkedIn receives more than 450 million page views per month, and more than 560,000 professionals visit the LinkedIn home page on an average day.

In this chapter, you learn to create and manage LinkedIn DirectAds. You can also listen to tips on getting the most from your LinkedIn advertising campaign and watch a video that shows you how to create an effective DirectAd.

Understanding LinkedIn Advertising Options

There are two advertising options on LinkedIn, each targeted to a specific advertising budget. These include

- **LinkedIn Advertising Sales.** This option is for companies with advertising budgets of $25,000 or more to place rich display advertising on LinkedIn. Ad products include a wide skyscraper, leaderboard, medium rectangle, and text link, all targeted to the exact demographic audience you want to reach. Figure 17.1 shows a sample ad.

- **LinkedIn DirectAds.** This option is for small businesses with advertising budgets as small as $50 to display low-cost text ads on LinkedIn. The LinkedIn DirectAds program is a self-service advertising option, similar to Google AdWords. You don't need to work with a sales representative to develop your advertising campaign. Instead, you enter your ad online and pay for it with a credit card. Figure 17.2 shows a sample text ad.

 TELL ME MORE   Media 17.1—LinkedIn Advertising Opportunities

Access this audio recording through your registered Web Edition at
my.safaribooksonline.com/9780789745095/media.

This chapter focuses on the self-service advertising with LinkedIn DirectAds. To learn more about LinkedIn advertising options for larger companies, click the Advertising link on the bottom navigation menu.

Figure 17.1   *An example of a medium rectangle ad on LinkedIn's home page.*

Figure 17.2   *You can create your own text ads to advertise to specific LinkedIn members.*

Working with LinkedIn DirectAds

It takes only a few minutes to set up a DirectAd, but it's a good idea to spend a bit more time analyzing your approach, content, and goals if you want to succeed. Here are some tips for creating DirectAds that generate results:

- **Because a text ad contains so few words, make every word count.** Your first effort will most likely contain too many words. Keep revising until you can communicate your message effectively within the ad length limitations.

- **Focus on a call to action.** You need to pique the interest of your target audience and encourage them to click your ad for more information.

- **Check your grammar and spelling.** Errors make your ad look unprofessional and reduce your click-through rate.

- **Verify that your URL works.** Even worse than grammar and spelling errors is a URL that doesn't work or leads to the wrong place.

- **Avoid using all capitalization in your ad.** Use title case for your headline and sentence case for your remaining ad.

- **Avoid ad content and topics that violate LinkedIn DirectAds Guidelines.** This includes ads for alcohol, tobacco, drugs, gambling, firearms, adult products, dating services, or multi-level marketing programs. Click the Advertising Guidelines link at the bottom of any LinkedIn DirectAds page to view the complete guidelines.

 SHOW ME   Media 17.2—Creating a LinkedIn DirectAd
Access this video file through your registered Web Edition at
my.safaribooksonline.com/9780789745095/media.

 LET ME TRY IT

Creating a LinkedIn DirectAd

To place a LinkedIn DirectAd, follow these steps:

1. Click the Advertising link on the bottom navigation menu.

2. Click the Start Advertising Now link in the LinkedIn DirectAds box. The Step 1 – Create Your Ad Campaign page opens, shown in Figure 17.3.

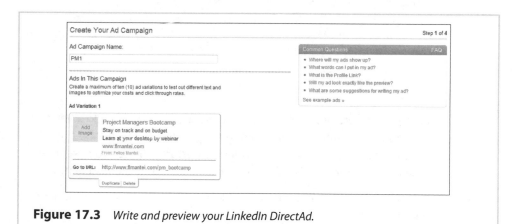

Figure 17.3 *Write and preview your LinkedIn DirectAd.*

3. In the Ad Campaign Name box, enter a descriptive name for your ad. This doesn't appear on your ad; it's for your reference only.

4. Enter a headline of up to 25 characters. Your headline is what draws members to your ad. Make it memorable and clear.

5. Enter up to 35 characters of text in line 1.

6. Enter up to 35 characters of text in line 2.

7. In the Display URL field, enter the URL to display on your ad.

8. Select your Profile Link from the drop-down list. You can display either your personal LinkedIn profile or a company profile.

You can't remove your profile link from your DirectAd; it's mandatory. LinkedIn doesn't allow anonymous ads.

9. In the Go to URL field, enter the landing page URL. A landing page refers to the page a visitor reaches after clicking a link in an online ad. Rather than directing visitors to a site's home page, most online marketers prefer to lead them to a specific page that directly relates to the clicked link. An online store, for example, could place a text ad for a particular product and lead visitors to a landing page that offers details about that product.

The two URL fields enable you to direct members who click your ad to a specific landing page on your site while displaying the URL of your site's home page on your actual ad. For example, your ad could display www.patricerutledge.com as the URL We Show, but lead visitors to www.patricerutledge.com/store/prod-uct234.htm as the URL We Go To. Note that the domain URL (www.patricerut-ledge.com) must be the same for both the display URL and the landing page URL.

10. If you want to create multiple variations of your ads, click the Add a Varia-tion link and complete the new ad. For example, you could change the headline or wording slightly to see which ad performs better. To save time, click the Duplicate link in your first ad to duplicate and then modify it.

11. Click the Next Step button to open the Step 2 – Target Your Audience page (see Figure 17.4).

12. If you don't want to target your ad, select the Show Ad to All LinkedIn Members option button. All LinkedIn members could potentially view your ad.

13. If you want to target your audience, select the Target Audience by Catego-ry option button. LinkedIn targets members based on their profile data, but their personal details are never available directly to advertisers. You can choose up to three categories. These include

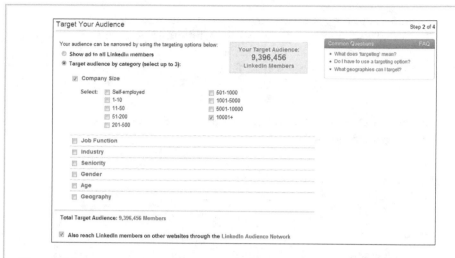

Figure 17.4 *Accurate targeting helps create a more successful ad.*

- **Company Size.** Select from nine options, ranging from self-employed members to members who work for companies with more than 10,000 employees.

- **Job Function.** Select up to 10 job functions. Options include Accounting, Creative, Human Resources, and Legal, as well as many others.

- **Industry.** Select up to 10 industries. These match the industry that appears on a LinkedIn member's profile.

- **Seniority.** Select the career levels of your target prospects. Options include Individual Contributor, Manager, Director, Vice President, Chief X Officer, or Owner.

- **Gender.** Select a gender (if your ad targets either a male or female audience).

- **Age.** Select the age ranges you want to target.

- **Geography.** Select a target geography. Options include the United States, Canada, India, Australia, Netherlands, or the United Kingdom. Within the United States, you can narrow your target audience to a specific metro area.

14. View the Total Target Audience field to see the effects of narrowing your audience. You can modify your criteria if the summary results don't match the audience size you want to reach.

15. If you want to display your ad on LinkedIn partner sites as well as LinkedIn.com, select the Also Reach LinkedIn Members on Other Websites Through the LinkedIn Audience Network checkbox.

Before continuing to the next page, review your target audience carefully. Consider who you want to reach and why. Is your estimated target audience too big or too small? Sometimes a small target audience can yield better results, but other times it just doesn't give you enough reach.

16. Click the Next Step button to open the Step 3 – Set Your Campaign Budget page, shown in Figure 17.5.

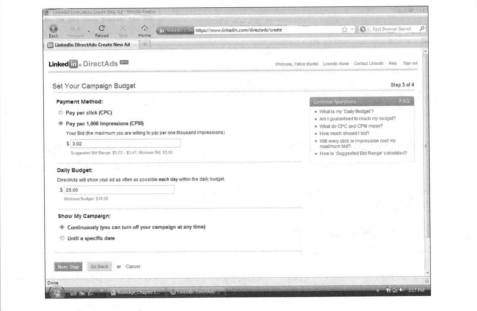

Figure 17.5   *Establish your budget and select a pricing model.*

17. Select the Pay per Click (CPC) option button if you want to pay based on the number of times a LinkedIn member clicks your ad. Enter the maximum amount you're willing to pay for each click. You might pay less per click depending on demand, but you won't pay more than this amount. LinkedIn displays a suggested range based on the current bids of other advertisers, but you can enter any amount you want over the minimum of $2.

CPC is a common online advertising term that stands for cost-per-click. When you choose a CPC advertising model, you pay only when someone clicks your ad.

18. Select the Pay per 1,000 Impressions (CPM) option button if you want to pay for every 1,000 impressions your ad receives. Enter the maximum amount you're willing to pay for each of the 1,000 impressions. You might pay less depending on demand, but you won't pay more than this amount. LinkedIn displays a suggested range based on the current bids of other advertisers, but you can enter any amount you want over the minimum of $3.

> CPM is a common online advertising term that stands for cost per thousand impressions. When you choose a CPM advertising model, you pay a fixed amount for every 1,000 ad impressions regardless of how many clicks it receives.

19. Enter the amount of money you're willing to spend each day in the Daily Budget field. LinkedIn continues to display your ad until you reach this limit. The minimum you can enter is $10.

20. Specify whether you want to show your campaign continuously or until a specified date. It's best to run a long-term campaign unless you're marketing something that's time-sensitive, such as an event.

21. Click the Next Step button to open the Billing Information page.

22. On this page, enter your personal and credit card information in the specified fields.

23. Click the Submit button to place your ad. LinkedIn charges your credit card $5 and credits this amount to your DirectAds account.

LinkedIn reviews your ad to verify that it meets its advertising guidelines. Until your ad is approved, its status is "Under Review."

Managing Your DirectAds

After receiving approval from LinkedIn, your ad will begin to appear on the LinkedIn site based on the targeted criteria you specify.

To manage your ads and view reports of your results, go to https://www.linkedin.com/directads/home to open the Manage Ads page.

This page has two tabs:

- **My Ad Campaigns.** This tab displays a summary of your results for each ad, such as your current budget, ad clicks, impressions shown, total click-through rate, average cost-per-click, and total spent. You can also turn your ads on

and off the LinkedIn network, hide them from the Summary tab, and copy
them to create a similar ad.

- **Reporting.** This tab, shown in Figure 17.6, provides reports that detail your
  impressions and clicks over specific time periods. You can download the
  reports in a CSV (comma separated values) format to import into applications
  such as Microsoft Excel.

Your click-through rate (CTR) tells you the percentage of people who clicked
your ad. Remember, however, that some people don't immediately click links in
ads; they do, however, visit website links that are shown in ads at a later time.

Figure 17.6   *Analyze your reporting data and adjust your DirectAds campaign if necessary.*

This chapter introduces several ways to access
LinkedIn using your mobile phone.

18

Accessing LinkedIn via Mobile Devices

Whether you use a Blackberry, iPhone, Palm Pre, Android, or another WAP-enabled phone, there's a way to access your LinkedIn data while you're on the go. In this chapter, you learn about LinkedIn Mobile as well as LinkedIn applications for the iPhone, Blackberry, and Palm Pre.

Using LinkedIn Mobile

LinkedIn Mobile enables you to view selected LinkedIn data and perform selected LinkedIn tasks on your mobile phone. If you use a Blackberry, iPhone, or Palm Pre, you should also consider the LinkedIn application specific to your phone.

 LET ME TRY IT

Accessing LinkedIn Mobile

To access LinkedIn on your mobile phone, follow these steps:

1. Point to http://m.linkedin.com.

2. Enter your email and LinkedIn password.

3. Click the Sign In button. Figure 18.1 shows LinkedIn Mobile.

4. Choose from the following options:
   - **0 Search.** Search by keywords, name, company, or title.
   - **1 Updates.** Update your status or view network updates of your connections.
   - **2 Contacts.** View summaries of your connections with links to their profiles and email.
   - **3 Profile.** View your profile.
   - **4 Invite.** Invite people to connect with you on LinkedIn.
   - **5 Settings.** Select your preferred language. Choices include English, German, Spanish, French, Japanese, or Chinese (either traditional or simplified).

Figure 18.1   *View LinkedIn profiles on your mobile phone.*

- **6 Feedback.** Provide feedback to LinkedIn.
- **7 Sign Out.** Sign out of LinkedIn.

Using the LinkedIn iPhone Application

LinkedIn offers a free application for the iPhone, shown in Figure 18.2, that's compatible with the iPod Touch and iPad and integrates with your iPhone address book. This application requires iPhone OS 3.0 or later. It's available in English, Chinese, French, German, Japanese, and Spanish.

For more information, visit http://www.apple.com/iphone/appstore/ or search the App Store in iTunes.

Using LinkedIn on Your Blackberry

LinkedIn for Blackberry enables you to work with your Blackberry contacts, calendar, and messaging. This application is available for Tour, Bold, and Curve using OS 4.3.0 or higher. To download LinkedIn for Blackberry, go to http://www.linkedin.com/blackberry.

Figure 18.2   *View LinkedIn network updates on your iPhone.*

Using LinkedIn on Your Palm Pre

If you own a Palm Pre, LinkedIn offers a free application in the Palm Pre application catalog. With this application, you can search and view profiles, send email to your connections, send invitations to connect, and view and accept outstanding invitations.

In addition, you can use Palm Synergy to sync the names, email addresses, and photos of your LinkedIn connections into your Palm Pre address book.

 LET ME TRY IT

Accessing LinkedIn on Your Palm Pre

To use Palm Synergy, follow these steps:

1. Open Contacts on your Pre.

2. Open the Application menu and select Preferences & Accounts.

3. Select Add an Account.

4. Select LinkedIn and log in to your LinkedIn account.

To learn more about LinkedIn Mobile options, go to
http://www.linkedin.com/static?key=mobile.

index